K 3
One So...

U.S. Army Horse Cavalry
China -Burma-India Theater
1943-1945

By
Donovan Dehner Ketzler

As told to
Vicki Krecek

Donovan Dehner Ketzler as told to Vicki Krecek

Contents

DEDICATION

This book is dedicated to all those heroes who fought and to the many who died so that we may live in freedom. While much is written on World War II, there is very little written about the China Burma India Theater. Perhaps one man's story will cast some light on that part of the Great War.

Preface

A group of friends were camping with their horses in the national forest near Chadron, Nebraska. One had a tent, two slept in their horse trailers, one in the back of his pickup, and one in the back of her dad's horse trailer. The days were hot, but the nights

Donovan Dehner Ketzler at 85 entered in 2009 U.S. Cavalry Association annual competition at Fort Robinson, Nebraska. He participated in mounted shooting, jumping and military horsemanship.

cool and everyone had relatively comfortable sleeping quarters, except for the rider sleeping in her father's horse trailer.

At the campfire, the young woman mentioned that bugs that flew in through the open trailer had pestered her all night. Donovan Ketzler, then in his late 70s and the oldest of the group by some margin, quietly got up and left the group. A few minutes later he returned and handed the young woman a fly net – large enough to cover the entire trailer.

This story is typical of Donovan "Van" Ketzler. He knows how to do things and seems to know and have on hand just what is needed in any situation. His pickup has a topper, where he can sleep on camping trips. A plywood "floor" rests on several four-by-fours, under which are tools, bug nets, and portable grills. The sides have an intricate bungee cord arrangement which holds water cans, fire extinguishers, and more tools. There is always a loaded pistol within reach and he wears a very sharp knife on his belt.

Here is a man who
- is always prepared;
- will never let himself be trapped;
- will always defend himself and his charges;
- is always optimistic and greets each new day as if it were a precious gift;
- and is very stubborn. When he wants to do something, he just does it.

I have been privileged to ride in his troop. Watching him, now at the age of 89, is like having a road map on how to reach a life fully lived. But what were the stops, turns and side roads that made such a man?

Growing up with a strong-willed, independent and worldly mother and a hard working father and grandfather who ran a boot

4

making company, Van learned a trade and responsibility at a young age. It was no surprise that as World War II broke out, he insisted on leaving college after only a month into his freshman year to enlist in the U.S. Army Horse Cavalry.

When I suggested that Van talk about his experiences in the U.S. Army Horse Cavalry and World War II, he quickly dismissed the idea saying, "I was no war hero." But he was a war hero. He was one of the people the Army counted on to get jobs done, one of the thousands of soldiers who carried out operations that helped win the war. This is the story, not of a decorated military leader, but of a man who was always prepared; never let himself be trapped; was always ready to defend his charges and himself; and who, with good humor, optimism and no small amount of stubbornness, figured out how to get things done to keep some part of the Army moving.

The U.S. Army's recruiting promotion, "Army of One," describes Donovan Ketzler's military service. As his son says, "Dad's guns are always loaded and his knives are always sharp." Ketzler was never assigned to any one unit. Rather, when he was stationed in Burma and China, he served where needed. In recounting these stories, he never mentioned the rugged conditions in the CBI. His are memories of the men and the jobs that needed to be done, and his stories are either positive or humorous. I have added those descriptions from accounts in the "Ex-CBI Roundup" to give some perspective of conditions.

Today, Ketzler may be the oldest member of the U.S. Army Horse Cavalry who still rides and jumps his horse.

Vicki Krecek

China-Burma India Theater WWII

Mars Task Force, Burma, WWII

Introduction

Officially established on March 3, 1942, the China-Burma-India Theater of Operations (CBI) is often referred to as the Forgotten Theater of World War II. Of the 12,300,000 Americans under arms at the height of World War II mobilization, relatively few, only about 250,000 (two percent) were assigned to the CBI Theater. Except for a few stories, CBI did not often make headlines in the newspapers back home. The 12,000-mile supply line, the longest of the war, was often last in line for supplies from the United States.

CBI was important to the overall war strategy. The Japanese had been invading Eastern China since the early 30s and had completely cut off China's sea access to the outside world. Occupation of Burma in 1942 by Japanese forces cut the last land supply line between China and the outside world. Keeping China in the war fighting the Japanese was important to the Allied war effort largely because it occupied so many Japanese troops. A military airlift was begun out of Ledo, Assam, in Northeast India in order to keep China supplied and in the war. But an airlift over the Himalayas would not be enough. A land supply route would be needed. A road from Ledo was begun in late 1942. Ledo was chosen because it was close to the northern terminus of a rail line from the ports of Calcutta and Karachi. Construction of the Ledo Road was completed in early 1945.

Allied forces in CBI, mostly British, Chinese, and Indian, engaged large numbers of Japanese troops that might have otherwise been used elsewhere. America's role in CBI was to support China by providing war materials and the manpower to get it to where it was needed. The Flying Tigers fought the Japanese in the air over China and Burma. Army Air Forces flew supplies Over the Hump from India to China. Merrill's Marauders fought through the jungles of

Burma. Army Engineers built the Ledo Road to open up the land supply route.

From an Allied military standpoint, the CBI was the end of the pipeline - the least important theater of operations in WWII. With the massive battles going on in Europe and the Pacific, priorities for military personnel and material dictated that only a trickle reach the CBI. The ground troops in CBI had to be extremely resourceful, flexible, and somewhat independent.

The Cavalry was trained to do a variety of jobs. Unlike troops in other services, branches, they were not specialists. They were trained in explosives, weapons and horsemanship. They were trained to handle just about any job in any situation. That made them valuable in the CBI. This is one soldier's story. Donovan Dehner Ketzler, K 37472591, was sent to the CBI at age 19. He served with a number of units but essentially was an independent soldier, assigned as needed. In many ways, he was an "Army of One."

The Army Horse Cavalry's Youngest Recruit

Growing up the son of a custom boot maker, Donovan Ketzler learned a trade at his dad's factory by the age of 12. He worked hard both at the factory and at school. Despite the hard work, as the owner's son also had a good deal of status. With the factory's seasoned craftsmen as tutors, he learned to cut and sew leather and make small leather items. The men at the factory looked at a problem as a challenge. Their example instilled in Van a belief that, if he thought it out, he could fix almost anything – particularly if it could be fixed with leather.

In addition to custom-made English riding boots, the factory made military boots, Sam Brown belts, and other military leather accessories. At that time, they also had a tailoring shop where they made custom military uniforms. Van's father, Harold "Bud" Ketzler enjoyed a good working relationship with the horsemen and military officers who were their customers, and became friends with the Army officers living at Fort Omaha.

Jan and Van Ketzler began riding with the US Cavalry at Fort Omaha where they learned military horsemanship, show jumping and care for horses.

One of those, Major Pop Good, was an avid and accomplished horseman. He believed that all Army Cavalry officers should also be good horsemen and required his men to ride at least two hours a day. There were 25 Army horses based at Fort Omaha and to keep them ridden on the weekends, Major Good (who was later a Master of Foxhounds at Fort Leavenworth Hunt) invited the officer's wives and children to take riding lessons.

Hearing about the weekend lessons, the elder Ketzler asked Major Good if his two children, Van and Janne could attend. The siblings learned to care for, as well as ride horses, all in the very strict, exacting military style. Van developed a great camaraderie with fellow students, particularly George Hoge. (Hoge's father later became a well-known General who took the famous bridge at Ramagan in WWII. A Bachelor Officers' Quarters at Fort Leavenworth is named in his honor.)

Frosty Morn, a beautiful chestnut with a great attitude, was the favorite horse of both George and Van, who convinced his mother to get him to the stables early to make sure he was able to

ride Frosty Morn. Many of the Army horses jumped well and were great and steady teachers as he developed his riding skills.

During the summer, Van was sent out to work on a Western cattle ranch in Wyoming and by age 14 he had become an accomplished rider. As he advanced, he rode in many shows around Western Iowa and Eastern Nebraska, including Ak-Sar-Ben. Van remembers those years fondly.

Lt. Bob Plumb

But the world was changing and Fort Omaha's days were numbered. A new General took over who thought the horses were a waste of time and money. He sent them to Troop A of the 113th Cavalry stationed in Council Bluffs. The stables were at 25th street, just south of Broadway.

* * *

The officers of Troop A rode every Sunday and invited the reserve officers from Omaha to join them. One of those officers, Bob Plumb, was an excellent horseman who knew Bud Ketzler well. He had seen Van's riding ability and offered to pick him up on Sunday mornings so he could ride with them.

Van was showing horses for the military when he was in high school.

So every weekend the teenager rode with the 113th Cavalry. He made himself indispensable to the officers by hopping off to open gates, picking up dropped bats (riding crops) and giving them a lead over particularly forbidding jumps as they rode in the steep bluffs overlooking the Missouri River. Van challenged them by jumping his horse off the top of the bluff, landing about 24 feet below, and then sliding the rest of the way down. (Today, at age 89, Van still challenges mounted police officers and friends to take steep slides and camelbacks.) At the bottom of the bluffs, they would cross the railroad tracks and gallop through the cottonwood trees, jumping logs and picking through dense brush. Van was always good for a lead over challenging jumps.

One of the officers, Joe Turner, owned a bar at 15th and Dodge Streets. Since Van was still dependent on a ride, he accompanied the troops on their trips to the bar after their Sunday rides, enjoying the hamburgers and the men's stories.

The summer was horse show season, and Van continued to be valuable to the troops. He rode Aztec, one of the finest jumping horses in the stable. As he was still under 18, he qualified for the junior class. That meant he could ride the officer's horses prior to their event, getting them familiar with the course and warming them up for the officers.

His deep seat and riding skills also contributed to the Troop A polo club. He wasn't asked to actually join the club, but he did play stick polo with them and proved valuable at riding off opposing riders and enabling his team to get to the ball and score.

Except for his age and civilian status, Van was becoming a regular cavalryman, participating in Troop A's regular military drills and learning about weapons. He received even more weapons and drilling training through the Central High School ROTC, where he was named Best Drill Officer.

* * *

12

World War II was looming and the military was rapidly changing in response. Van was just 17 when the country federalized the National Guard, and his days of riding with Troop A ended abruptly when it was moved out of Council Bluffs. The weekend after the Troop moved, Van took a streetcar over to Council Bluffs to check on the stables. As he approached he saw about 20 horses all lying down asleep. But when he got closer, it hit him. The horses weren't sleeping. They were dead. All of them shot in the head. It was a scene he would never forget.

The stable was a sign of the changing times. The U.S. was still coming out of the depression and war was threatening. Horses were a luxury people could not afford. Younger horses were sent to remount stations but, since there was no market for surplus Army mounts, all horses over age seven were shot.

Induction into the U.S. Army Horse Cavalry

Hitler was threatening all of Europe and Japan was trying to become a world power in Asia and the Pacific. On Sunday morning, Dec. 7, 1941, the Japanese attacked the U.S. Pacific fleet based in Pearl Harbor, Guam and Wake and Midway islands. The United States declared War. U.S. citizens were enraged at the attack and men of all ages rushed to sign up for the Armed Services.

Van graduated from high school in 1942 and wanted to enlist immediately. His parents insisted he first go to college, so that fall, he headed for the University of Nebraska in Lincoln. He didn't last a month. He had already spent years training with the military. In his heart and mind, he was already a Cavalryman. He belonged fighting with his troops, not in college. Van called his father and said he just had to go. College could wait.

At that time, if you volunteered for induction rather than wait to be drafted, you were allowed to choose the branch of the service.

Freshman, University of Nebraska

Van went out to Fort Omaha and signed up for the U.S. Army Horse Cavalry. When they questioned his choice and suggested he might like the Air Corps, Van was adamant. "Horse Cavalry."

It was the day before Thanksgiving and Van went to Fort Omaha with close friends Buzzy Howard (who later married Susie Storz), Pete Petello and Bob Wilkerson. The four were given physicals and told to report to Fort Crook (Now Offutt Air Force Base) the morning after Thanksgiving. But Buzzy's mother, who worked at the induction center, said he had a heart murmur, so he was rejected. Instead, he spent the entire war building the Alaskan Highway. The remaining three reported to Fort Crook on a Friday morning. That afternoon they boarded a train for Fort Des Moines Induction Center, where Ketzler was assigned a number – 37472591 – his designation throughout WWII.

The three 18 year-olds reported to Fort Des Moines filled with patriotism and pride in their country, only to be dressed in oversized heavy wool clothes that smelled strongly of moth balls. When Van said the coat was too tight, he was told not to worry, it would soon fit. When he commented that his pants were too long, he was told to roll them up. It was hardly the image he remembered of the dashing officers who came into the factory. Van also remembers serving as a guinea pig for a trainee practicing vaccinations. After several attempts to insert the needle in Van's arm, the trainee finally succeeded – and the supervising doctor promptly told the trainee to try it again.

There were attempts made to boost morale at the Induction Center, including dances: every fourth recruit was tapped for attendance and on one occasion, Ketzler was the fourth man. The Center also served as a WAC induction center, so there was no shortage of women, but since their uniforms were as ill-fitting and smelling as the young men's, they were as equally withdrawn. Needless to say there wasn't much dancing, but that was OK with Ketzler since he never had liked to dance.

From Fort Des Moines, the recruits were ordered to training facilities for the various services. Ketzler was ordered to an infantry training center at Camp Irwin in California. But that wasn't what he had signed on for. He marched into the Sergeant to protest. When the Sergeant said he couldn't do anything, the 18-year-old demanded to see the Major. Insisting that he had signed up voluntarily and was therefore allowed to pick his service, Ketzler said he wanted to be assigned to the Horse Cavalry. The Major changed the orders. Two days later, Ketzler was on a train to Fort Riley, Kansas.

Fort Riley – Basic Training – Horse Cavalry

His recruiting class was an interesting mixture of men from all over the U.S. Many were horsemen who had also requested the Horse Cavalry. Ketzler remembers one was a jockey, and particularly mean. He was very small and wouldn't take any guff from anyone. Another, Bob Nichols was an 8-goal professional polo player from San Antonio, Texas. Another classmate was Whitey Powell, a stunt rider from Hollywood.

Few men describe basic training as "a piece of cake," but Ketzler had been through the drills since age 12. He knew military drilling, military etiquette, military horse care and horsemanship, and weapons. He had trained on the '03 Springfield rifle at Central High School ROTC. He knew the weapons manuals. Ketzler stood out because he could practically instruct the very training he was supposed to be learning.

Basic training is a 13-week course. The first month cadets received weapons training and learned Army discipline, etiquette, precautions, safety and enthusiasm. They were sent to movies warning of the dangers of venereal disease and building enthusiasm - "Why We Fight."

Before each payday, the men were called for a "Short Arm Inspection." They were ordered to fall out and return in ten minutes.

The uniform was boots, raincoats and helmet liners – nothing else. The men would parade by the doctor, open the raincoat and be

inspected for venereal disease. If there was any evidence of it, they didn't get paid. Ketzler remembers after the war seeing the movie *Battleground,* starring Van Johnson. In one scene, two people were talking in the foreground, but in the background was a group of soldiers dressed in boots, raincoats and helmet covers – nothing else. He said all the Vets in the theater burst into laugher. No one else had any idea why they were laughing.

At Fort Riley

* * *

Ketzler's drill Sergeant was a Texan by the name of Joe Nanny. On the first day of class, he stood before the recruits and said, "My name is Joe Nanny. J.O.E. N.A.N.N.Y. I am the stud Duck here. If you want to f---, fight or fool around, you've got to see me first."

16

Nanny became a role model for Ketzler who remembers the drill sergeant as a nice guy, tough but very fair, and he always looked after his men. No one mistreated his people.

Finally, after four weeks of basic training, they started horsemanship. Initially it was groundwork – caring for the horses, grooming and hauling manure. After a week they were allowed to ride. The men were taught a deep seat and good balance by trotting, without stirrups or reins, in a small circle for two hours. They rode in a building called the "sweat box" because the low metal ceiling and manure floor made it quite hot. When an exhausted recruit fell off a horse, soldiers on ground crew quickly hoisted him back on. But before the two hours were up, men were intentionally falling off their horses just to get a break. In addition to balance and a deep seat, the men learned a very important survival technique – how to fall and not get hurt.

3-4 Platoon Troop A, 1st Sq. C.R.T.C., Fort Riley 3-8-1943

The drill instructor for horsemanship was Count Oleg Cassini – later to become a famous fashion designer. He actually was titled, and the men liked to tease him by calling him "Count." But Cassini was very proud of being a part of the U.S. Army, and insisted on being called Corporal. So the troops good-naturedly referred to him as "Count Corporal."

Cassini had quite a bit of money and mingled with the Hollywood crowd. His mother, the countess, and wife, movie star Jean Tierney, were living nearby in Junction City and one day, Cassini and his wife gave a party for officers at Fort Riley. One woman came who had measles and exposed Tierney, who was three months pregnant. Sadly, she later gave birth to a baby with deformities.

Cassini trained them in horsemanship, one platoon (36 men) at a time. He soon discovered Ketzler was a competent, military-trained horseman, so he frequently pulled him off to help with a recruit having problems. One week into training, at morning roll call, the Sergeant ordered "Ketzler, front and center." His mind immediately searched for what he might have done wrong. The Sergeant barked that all the men were going to become Horse Cavalrymen or he would die trying. But one man had excelled and had already earned his spurs – Private Ketzler. The 19-year-old was the first to earn his spurs and be recognized as a Horse Cavalryman. He wore them proudly and they still hang in his office.

* * *

Ketzler's commanding officer, Captain "Razor Blade" Barnes was a "mustang," a man who had been a sergeant in many places and had come up through the ranks. He had about 20 years in the Army, and provided another role model for Ketzler.

When Barnes handed out a promotion, his first order was for the trooper to buy two small aspirin tins. He then ordered him to dump out the aspirin, put a piece of blitz cloth in one tin and a razor blade in the other. The blitz cloth was to polish their brass buttons whenever they had a break. When Barnes asked to see the aspirin boxes, the blitz cloth had better be dirty from use. The razor blade was to remind them that Barnes had given them their stripes; the trooper could sew them on, but Barnes could easily take them away.

The Captain was a great scavenger and his men benefited from his efforts. Other platoons might go wanting, but Barnes' men always had jelly on the table. He made a point of asking other troop commanders what they needed, and then procuring that item to trade for things his own men needed. Since machine gun barrels were always in demand, Barnes had gathered up old ones thrown in the dump. Then he directed the men on barracks cleaning duty to polish them, rubbing the barrels until they were hot.

It took about 10 hours of rubbing to get the rust off and restore them to "new" condition.

* * *

Fort Riley, Home for 20 months

Barnes was in charge of six platoons of 36 men each, so he didn't get to know many of the men personally – but he did get to know Ketzler. Once, during a bivouac, Barnes and some other officers tried to get a campfire going to heat their morning coffee, but the wood was soggy from being on the wet ground and wouldn't start. Ketzler watched as they unsuccessfully tried several times and then offered to help. He picked dead branches off the trees, as he had learned in Boy Scouts. Since they hadn't been on the ground, they were still dry and the fire started immediately. The officers soon had their morning coffee.

Captain Barnes knew Ketzler was an excellent horseman and once asked Van to accompany him on a ride to inspect a bridge that was to be blown up in the next day's explosives demonstration. Barnes rode a beautiful but young horse he was in the process of training.

As they neared the bridge, the horse spooked and whirled. Barnes landed on the ground and the horse ran back to the stable. Ketzler quickly offered the Captain his mount. "Ketzler, don't ever give up your horse," Barnes barked. "You are a Cavalryman. Without your horse, you're nothing but a damned infantryman."

(Ketzler learned that lesson well. He has torn four rotator cuffs, two on each side, since age 70. Each time it happened, he was leading a horse that jumped away from him – and he refused to let go.) So Ketzler followed on horseback while the Captain walked. With each step, he hit his riding crop and his boot and said, "I got tossed." He was very mad.

* * *

After the first two months of basic training, the recruits were allowed to leave on Saturday after maneuvers and return Sunday night. Ketzler took the opportunity to head back to Omaha. He could usually hitch a ride home and then, on Sunday, take a bus to Lincoln in order to catch the midnight bus back to Junction City. There were many recruits returning on that bus, and he often had to stand for the five-hour trip. The bus dropped him off around 5 a.m. at a stop about a mile from his barracks. If he ran, he could just make it for 5:30 reveille.

He probably would have gone back to Omaha nearly every weekend if it weren't for polo, which Barnes liked to play. He caught up with Ketzler on a Saturday morning and mentioned that they were going to play polo on Sunday. Ketzler said that he was going home, but the Captain merely said that the game would start at 10 a.m. – "Be there."

At the time, officers could keep their personal horses by an arrangement with the Army. The officer would "sell" their horse to the Cavalry for $1, which the officer would refund later when he left the service. Captain Barnes had three of his own mounts; the beautiful young horse which threw him; a solid trooper horse; and a polo pony. Nichols, the professional polo player, rode his green horse, Ketzler rode the trooper horse, and Barnes rode the polo pony. Ketzler's talent was in riding off the opposing team member, leaving Nichols to gain control of the ball and pass it to the Captain, who would come in for the score.

* * *

A field-mounted review with 2,000 mounted horses on the parade field, Ketzler remembers, was a beautiful sight. It wasn't long before Barnes asked him to be his guidon bearer and carry the Company's flag. It was a tremendous honor – Ketzler was just a 19-year-old recruit, but he would accompany the Captain in front of the entire company.

In a review, when the Adjutant called "Officers Front and Center," the captains and their guidon bearers galloped to the front of the field in a line up. Captain Barnes told Ketzler that he was always first at the front, and he expected Ketzler to be fast and right beside him.

As the adjutant began to say "Officers…" Ketzler saw Barnes kick his horse – hard. Ketzler did the same. Both horses leapt some twenty feet forward. When the Captain reached the front and saluted, Ketzler, immediately beside him, lowered the guidon close to the Captain's ear. They were definitely first. Barnes didn't smile much, but Ketzler could tell he was tremendously pleased. From then on Ketzler was his guidon bearer.

A Private – Acting Drill Sergeant

When he finished basic training, Ketzler was ordered to the 124th Cavalry, the only operating Horse Cavalry unit in the country, to patrol the Texas-Mexican border. But when he and Whitey Powell boarded the train at 3 a.m., Captain Barnes suddenly appeared and ordered them both off the train. He said their orders to Texas were rescinded. Barnes had gotten a new troop and needed good men to train them, specifically Ketzler and Powell. Within five days both had barracks and were acting drill sergeants in charge of 36 men – while still privates.

Ketzler was then just 19 and training men much older, most of whom didn't volunteer for the Horse Cavalry. But Joe Nanny had taught them well and was still around, happy to give advice. Ketzler had some trouble with authority at first, but eventually just worked it out.

Powell and Ketzler were selected as drill sergeants because they knew what to do. Neither man disappointed anyone.

After 15 weeks, Captain Barnes told Powell and Ketzler that he had received authorization for a Corporal position, with another position in a week. Meanwhile, he said, why didn't the two just flip a coin to see who would receive the first promotion. Powell won and Ketzler made Corporal the next week.

To celebrate their new positions, Captain Barnes suggested they take the horses and ride down to Ogden's Inn. Once there, they proceeded to get very drunk. When the bar closed, the bartender loaded them back on their horses and sent them home. It was seven miles home but the horses knew the way, so the two fell asleep. When they returned, the stable night guard put the horses away and the two new Corporals slept on the ground.

* * *

Kansas is prone to weather extremes. Hot summers, bitter cold winters, tornados and flash floods. In the spring of 1944, Ketzler had his group out on a bivouac in a simulated battle with another troop. That night they camped with about 20 men and horses on Three Mile Creek. It looked as if it might rain so Ketzler picked a soft spot in the dry creek bed and used the two packsaddles to make a tent over himself. He woke up to feel a wet blanket. It was sprinkling lightly, but it appeared the water was coming from the ground. Just then, one of the men ran over and yelled that the creeks were starting to flow and rising fast. Ketzler jumped up, yelled at the men to get their equipment and weapons, including machine guns, to higher ground. He put on his three-buckle boots and helmet, ran to the picket line, grabbed the lead ropes of all 20 horses and led them to the high ground beside the creek.

The piece of high ground on which Ketzler ended up was between two creek beds. He was quickly marooned on an island flanked by creeks some 9 feet deep with raging floodwater. There he stood, dressed only in boots, helmet and skivvies, pistol strapped on, holding 20 horses, while his men watched helplessly from across the creek.

Thankfully, the water in the creek went down almost as fast as it had risen. Van's troop had lost a lot of equipment, including their saddles and bridles. But they had saved the horses, men, and most of the weapons. But a troop of black soldiers, camped further downstream, was not so fortunate. They were caught off guard and as a result lost three men.

Van's men rode their horses with just their lead shanks to search for the remaining equipment and were able to salvage quite a bit. The next day they brought trucks to pick it up. Ketzler lost all his clothes, so he rode back in his boots, skivvies and britches with his pistol strapped underneath. When the Army asked for an accounting of what was lost, Ketzler reported the pistol missing. For the remainder of the War, that .45 pistol never left his side.

One spring afternoon, Ketzler was out on an obstacle course with a group of trainees. It was a clear, sunny day, but extremely hot and still. They were up in the flint hills above their camp at Republican Flats when, suddenly, out of nowhere, it began to rain and hail. They scrambled up to the top of the bluffs overlooking their barracks area. A tornado was headed right for the camp. It cut in by the stables and along the side of the large barn. It destroyed some of the corral fences, but seemed to leave the barn intact. Then it headed over to the mess hall. They watched the whole building disappear almost instantly. The tornado continued and missed the main barracks, but flattened several of the temporary barracks shacks where Ketzler and his men were staying. It went through the camp then followed the Republican River downstream. At their position on the top of the bluffs, it was a sunny day so they had a clear view of the tornado.

Ketzler and his men rushed down to see about the horses. They were all in their stalls eating contently, as if nothing had happened. A huge, very heavy manure spreader had been lifted and tossed several hundred yards away. The mess hall was destroyed, but most of the men on KP duty had taken cover in the large cooler, which was the only thing left standing. One KP soldier who didn't make it to the cooler was killed. Ketzler's temporary barracks building was flattened. Although his cot was a tangled mess of steel wrapped around his mattress, his boots were still standing by the bedside, completely undisturbed.

* * *

Ketzler encountered several celebrities while at Fort Riley. Many, like Mickey Rooney, went through a shortened "basic training" course and then went to various areas as morale boosters for the troops. Ketzler especially remembers boxer Joe Louis. A very handsome man, Louis had fantastic eye-hand coordination. He also had some physical assets that helped make him a world-class boxer, including longer than normal arms, very large hands and a lightning fast response. While Ketzler trained the boxer in firing a .45-caliber pistol, Louis would fire the weapon, quickly reach around behind his back with his left hand, and snatch the spent cartridge out of the air. Everyone loved it – except Ketzler's superior. He thought Louis was showing off and wanted Ketzler to put a stop to it. But the young corporal felt it was harmless; a great display of physical ability, and good for the morale of the black troops. Ketzler let Louis continue the feat.

Although Trooper Vashon wasn't a celebrity, he certainly was a man to be remembered. A French Canadian from Maine, Vashon didn't speak English when he was drafted, so he attended a special school before he was sent to Fort Riley. He was an excellent marksman, but wouldn't engage the safety lock on his weapon. It was a point of contention with Ketzler, but Vashon told him that if he was driving down a highway and a deer darted across the road, he would have enough time to grab his rifle, but not to take off the safety.

Waking Vashon in the morning was an interesting affair, Ketzler remembers. He would try to get him up and Vashon would ask, "Are we going to ride ze horses today?" If Ketzler said no, Vashon would ask, "Are we going to shoot ze weapons today?" If the answer was still a no, Vashon would pull the covers over his head. Ketzler would then have to turn the bed over to get him up. But if the answer to either question was yes, Vashon would be the first out of bed.

The proper position for target shooting was to lay prone on the ground, using a sling to steady the shooting arm. Vashon refused to use a sling because he said it got in his way. Ketzler insisted on the sling, but when he turned away, Vashon would simply take it off. Captain Barnes told Ketzler that Vashon had to comply. Still Vashon refused.

One day at target practice, in order to prove the worth of the sling, Barnes, who was an excellent marksman, challenged Vashon. Barnes fired first, using the sling, and hit five perfect shots in the center of the target. Vashon, without the sling, also put five shots into the center. Barnes said the target was pretty close, so they moved the whole group back to fire at 300 yards. (Moving the group back meant moving about thirty gun stands and 300 men, so the Lieutenant in change wasn't thrilled about it.) At 300 yards, Barnes again hit five bull's eyes. Vashon, without the sling, also hit five bull's eyes. So, Barnes told him he would absolutely have to have the sling at 500 yards. That was close to a third of a mile, and further than they ever practiced target shooting. (At this point, the Lieutenant was becoming very agitated. He had a time schedule to follow and the impromptu shooting match was totally disrupting it.) Now at 500 yards, Barnes hit the exact center on three shots, and right on the line with two. But Vashon, without the sling, again placed all five in the center. Adding insult to injury, Vashon told him it was easy to hit the target lying down. He then stood up, shouldered the rifle, and hit another five in the center of the target. Captain Barnes told Ketzler to let Vashon fire as he wanted.

* * *

A week after the first group of recruits graduated Ketzler received another group of 36 men. By the end of Ketzler's second group of recruits, he was officially promoted and so trained the third group through as a Sergeant.

His third group of recruits was on field exercises engaged in guerrilla work. Ketzler supervised the setting up of camp and picket lines. They were ready to cook some chow when Ketzler decided to check one of the outposts. He grabbed a horse off the picket line and jumped on it with just the halter and rode up to the top of the hill. The climb was exceptionally steep and near the top, the horse turned suddenly and ran down to the bottom. Ketzler grabbed a bridle for more control over the horse. When he reached the same spot on the hill, the horse did the same thing. Ketzler reached down on his neck and jumped back on his loins. The horse gave a toss and Ketzler went over his head. It resulted in a flurry of legs as the horse tried to gain his footing on the steep hill. He tried not to step on Ketzler and Ketzler tried to get out of his way, but didn't quite make it.

When he finally returned to camp for chow, Ketzler's shoulder was in excruciating pain. The cook was going back with the truck and gave him a ride to the hospital, where he was told he had a broken scapula and ordered to bed until the doctor could see him in the morning.

The next day was a little slow so some of the non-coms, including Whitey Powell and Bobby Egan came over to visit

Ketzler. As a sergeant, he was given a private room on a screened porch, which the guys rode right up onto so their horses could put their heads through the window.

Egan had just gotten a new horse and Ketzler decided he wanted to try it out. He jumped through the window, got on the horse and galloped him down to the end of the road and back several times. The nurse discovered him missing and flew out the double screen door, screaming at him to get off that horse. Close behind her came an equally upset doctor.

When Ketzler got back to bed, the Doctor took his shoe and drew an imaginary line all the way around the bed, saying that this was a line Ketzler could not cross that line. It was a couple of weeks before he was able to return to duty.

* * *

Horses were rapidly becoming obsolete in warfare. The cavalry was discontinuing its horsemanship training and rapidly becoming mechanized. But the First Cavalry was in the Pacific Islands, and wanted horse people who were resourceful and dependable. The Cavalry soldier knew how to repair, load and fire weapons ranging from a pistol to a mortar. They were trained to blow up bridges, handle machine guns and build camps. They knew how to take care of their pack and riding animals, and could do their own messing. This was not true of other service branches, where most soldiers were trained as specialists. Also, Cavalry troops were trained that their job didn't end when they returned from a mission – they had a horse to care for. It was a big responsibility.

The war was intensifying and more men were needed fast – it was a waste of time to train men through the horse cavalry. Ketzler's last group to finish basic training was the last group trained in horse cavalry. All the non-commissioned officers at Fort

Riley, about 60 including Ketzler, were ordered to Fort Ord, California.

The National Guard units were being called up and were now mechanized. Since they had a large amount of surplus horse equipment, it was sent it to Fort Riley. There were now piles of bridles, saddles and other equipment for which there was no longer any use. When Ketzler took the opportunity to go home before heading to Fort Ord, a friend of his, a supply sergeant, filled up the back end of Ketzler's car with saddles, bridles and other equipment. He still has much of the equipment, which otherwise would have been discarded.

Fort Ord, California

It was a three-day train ride from Kansas City to Fort Ord, where Ketzler and many of the other Horse Cavalry non-coms were assigned. They rode in cattle cars with large Dutch doors. The top door was kept open the whole way. When Ketzler learned the train would stop in Reno, he called an Omaha friend who was attending school there and suggested she come down. She did, and brought three carloads of her sorority sisters. Ketzler jumped off the train to give her a hug, and the rest of the girls quickly made friends with the soldiers. His status with the other men took a great leap.

Barracks at Fort Ord

Since they got in to San Francisco at 2 a.m., they were given the next day to explore the city. The non-coms headed for the YMCA, took an early morning swim and promptly filled the pool with empty whiskey bottles.

The next morning they decided to split up in order to explore the city. Ketzler walked about two blocks and discovered a burlesque theatre. He bought a ticket and some popcorn and settled in to watch the movie. Suddenly on the screen was a girl he had known from Fort Riley, who had told the men she was a movie star. Ketzler let out a whoop – "Holly cow, this is where she is a movie star!" His outburst got a quick response from a number of others in the audience. It turned out that most of the Fort Riley guys from the train had discovered the same theater. What the heck, they thought – they all moved over and sat together to watch their "movie star" from Fort Riley.

* * *

Fort Ord, in Monterey, was one of the largest army bases on the West Coast. It was a beautiful setting and is the current home of California State University Monterey Bay.

There were some 250 Horse Cavalry men from Fort Riley at Fort Ord when Ketzler reported. They underwent intensive outdoor training. It was early winter, and the coastal weather was tough on the Midwesterners. It was icy cold at 5 a.m. so they put on heavy coats. At exactly 11 a.m. the sun burned off the fog and it turned very hot. At lunch they shed their heavy coats and went back in the field. At 4 p.m., again on the dot, it turned cold again.

Ketzler was extremely allergic to poison ivy, which would spread rapidly over his body. Unfortunately he had the same reaction to poison oak, which could be found throughout the valleys of the rough coastal range. He was miserable. It spread all over his body and was particularly bad in the crotch. To keep from scratching himself raw, he slept with the big gloves he had been issued for the Kansas winters.

The next morning he asked the doctor for a shot of the medicine he knew would arrest it, but the doctor told him all he needed was Calamine lotion. Ketzler told the doctor he might as well flush the lotion down the toilet for all the good it would do him. But the doctor refused to prescribe anything else. That night Ketzler went to the dispensary where he knew the CQ in charge. The CQ found three vials of the medicine Ketzler needed, but neither man knew how to give a shot. Ketzler just drank all three vials. It eliminated most of the symptoms of the poison oak, but it seemed to concentrate in his knee, which became enormously swollen. He couldn't get his britches on, so that night he sat in a sink and let cold water run on the knee until morning. It worked, and the swelling went down enough to let him get the britches on. By evening, it took two guys to help get them off.

The men from the Horse Cavalry were the only ones in britches and boots, so the others referred to them as "Western Union" guys. Ketzler remembers that the Paratroopers were crazy and liked to jump out of windows. When they had morning roll call, the Paratroopers would jump out of the second story windows. When they hit the ground, they would buckle their knees, roll forward and then jump in the line for inspection.

Fort Ord was a beautiful place, with a club called The Stilwell Club, overlooking Monterey Bay. On any evening some 400-500 soldiers would be there, drinking 50 cent pitchers of beer. One night a riot broke out when a Paratrooper stood on a table and said "F*** the Cavalry." A Cavalryman then jumped on the table and declared that it took a pretty good man to stay on a horse, but any dumb SOB could fall out of airplanes. A glass of beer hit him on the cheek. The MPs were called to break up the riot.

Riverside, California

Ketzler and the others from Fort Riley left Fort Ord for Camp Anza in Riverside, California. It was a final deployment before going overseas. The men were given physicals and more shots. Since Ketzler's knee was still very swollen, they put him in the hospital where it could be treated and iced. Each night the nurse would come in, pull up the covers from the bottom of the bed, and massage the knee and change the ice packs.

On the second night, a new nurse came – a young, good-looking blond second lieutenant. When she came to change his ice pack, she pulled his sheet down from the top, leaving Ketzler lying naked and exposed. Not seeming to notice, she rubbed the knee and changed the ice pack. The sight of this lovely young woman working over his naked body caused him to become aroused. Meanwhile, the rest of the men in the ward who could walk moved in to get a closer look at the second lieutenant. But when they saw Ketzler, they fell silent. Ketzler remembers, "You could hear a pin drop."

When the nurse finished, she whipped out a pencil from behind her ear, gave his erect member a sharp whack, pulled up the sheet, and walked out to uproarious laughter. The next morning, the doctor looked at Ketzler's knee and said, "Get out of here – you're fine."

Ketzler never learned whether the doctor had heard about the incident.

With the knee under control, Ketzler had one free evening before going overseas. He called Char Wilsie, a friend from Omaha attending UCLA and invited her to dinner. Ten dollars was all the money he had and he used it to take the train to LA and buy dinner. They ordered cokes because they were not old enough to drink. Ketzler had a great time on his last night in America.

Shipped Overseas

The next morning the men boarded a 5 a.m. train headed for San Pedro, near Long Beach. Troop movement during wartime was confidential so every window on the train was blacked out. The train pulled up to the dock and the men were hustled a few steps to the gangplank leading to their ship, The General John Pope, a large troop transport which carried 5,000 soldiers. The men were immediately sent below decks to what would be their quarters for the next 35 days.

Ketzler shared cramped quarters with 500 men, three decks below sea level, in the ship's stern. He was put in charge of 50 of them. Their bunks were in vertical stacks of four, each with only about 24 inches between. Ketzler had rank and claimed a top bunk, which had a little more headroom and allowed him to watch the whole room.

The men weren't allowed on deck until the ship was five miles out to sea. When they came up, they could see the coast of California fading away in the distance. It was a pretty sight, but the men enjoyed it just a short time. The waters along the West Coast are extremely rough, especially in winter, and the men became very seasick. The black troops quartered in the ship's bow suffered the most, as that was the roughest ride on the ship.

Ketzler remembered everyone was sick. If you didn't get sick from the motion, you got sick watching others be sick. In the mess hall, men would take trays of food to long narrow tables where they stood to eat. One night, across the table from Ketzler, a black soldier became sick and vomited onto his tray. The soldier just pushed it aside and continued eating. Ketzler nearly lost his own dinner and quickly ran up to the deck for some cold night air.

The latrine in Ketzler's quarters was in the stern, directly above the propellers. The soldiers could sit on the stool and look down onto the propellers. In rough seas, the ship would heave way up and then slam down,

General John Pope WWII Troop Transport

forcing water up through the hole. If someone was sitting on it at that time, he got hit with seawater. During storms, the latrine was full of water – not all of it from the ocean.

* * *

Every soldier had a shipboard duty. The Air Corps supplied the gun crews, the Navy manned the guns and the Fort Riley Cavalrymen pulled K.P. As Ketzler's group from Fort Riley hadn't been paid in three months but the Air Corps and Navy had just received their pay, it became a challenge to the Cavalry to obtain money from the other service branches. Since the Cavalry controlled the food and food service, they decided to short everyone's rations just a little. There were only two items, breakfast and dinner, so the men quickly got hungry. The Cavalry had one of the men serve up the meals, which left an extra man to go back and make "jam sandwiches" (a piece of meat and a piece of cheese jammed between two slices of bread). During the day, the Cavalry would peddle the jam sandwiches for 50 cents each. Ketzler remembers it was robbery, but the guys were hungry and happy to pay. The Cavalrymen expanded their earnings even more by beating the others at cards.

Melbourne, Australia

The General John Pope traveled at about 20 knots, faster than submarines. So, even though it was wartime, the men crossed the Pacific Ocean without an escort. They traveled far to the south to avoid the active combat zones in the Pacific. Thankfully, the crossing was uneventful except for the rough seas. The ship pulled into Port Phillip Bay, Melbourne two weeks after it had departed California. Melbourne is located a good distance inland on a back bay and traveling through the sound to get there was a beautiful trip.

As the ship approached the dock, the soldiers spotted another beautiful sight in the form of a lovely Australian girl, a WAF, standing on the dock checking something on a clipboard. The men all wanted a look, but just then, General Alarm sounded and all the men returned immediately to quarters. When they were locked in, the Captain announced over the PA system that the men, by gathering all on one side, almost turned the ship over. He said he understood their enthusiasm, but cautioned that if this were to happen again, he would be forced to lock them below decks the entire time they were in Melbourne. The doors were opened and the men went back onto the deck, this time carefully spreading all around the ship. Of course, the pretty young woman was long gone.

No one was allowed off the ship for the five days they were in port. Race riots were erupting in Melbourne, and because the ship had 700 black troops, no one was allowed off. The race riots began when Australian soldiers, returning from the war, found the American black troops had taken their girls. The black troops, the 9th Cavalry, were originally assigned up in the islands, the Marshals and Bougainville, but they hadn't worked out as soldiers. Ketzler said they had wonderful non-commissioned officers, but for whatever reason, the black enlisted men wouldn't fight. Ketzler said he didn't

OVER-PAID
OVER-SEXED
OVER HERE?
U.S. MARINES IN WARTIME
MELBOURNE 1943

Exhibition Dates 17 February – 30 April 2010

know why they wouldn't fight – it could have been the attitude of the whites. So they were pulled out of the islands and sent back to Australia to unload ships, drive trucks, and work as quartermasters and stevedores. They wooed the Australian women by telling them they were the "true" Native Americans.

Meanwhile the Australian soldiers were returning from a major victory in Africa, but one that came with heavy casualties.

They had fought the major battles of El-Alamein and Tobruk and chased German General Rommel back across Africa. The Australians were sent home jubilant, but exhausted, for a well-deserved rest. When they discovered that 'American Indians' were wooing their girls, they started the race riots.

***

From an hour before sundown until an hour after sunrise, Ketzler's men were locked in their quarters and not allowed topside; enemy subs could creep close to the ship under cover of darkness, and could see the men silhouetted on deck.

Sailing from Australia to India, the men enjoyed the sunshine and played cards. They even held an equator-crossing party, complete with King Neptune. But it wasn't always smooth sailing.

Once, the men were in their quarters when they heard a loud explosion and then saw what appeared to be a wall of water coming at them. The lights below were all red, so it was difficult to see, but everyone thought a torpedo had hit the ship. The men started to panic. The doors all slammed shut and locked. Ketzler ordered his men to put on their boots and get their canteens. He wanted to keep them occupied and knew if they had to abandon ship, they would need boots and canteens. At all times, the men had two full canteens and wore a life vest, which they could blow up if needed.

Suddenly, Ketzler realized that it was not water, but steam, coming through their quarters. He quickly assured the men that they were not hit and they were going to be all right. A five-inch steam pipe had broken.

Four first sergeants had panicked. They left their men and were pounding at the door to get out. One broke his hand pounding so hard. They were all demoted to private.

The ship's officers came down to reassure the men. Some of the men suffered steam burns, but no other harm was done. And, though it could have been worse, "it scared the shit out of all of us," Ketzler said.

There was an even darker side to their journey. It came via the radio and the voice of Tokyo Rose. The Japanese broadcaster seemed to know everything about them, where the ship was, how many men were on it, and that it sailed from Melbourne and was headed to Bombay. Her harassment unnerved the men.

The real attack came about four days later, in the middle of the Indian Ocean, when Japanese planes attacked the ship. General Quarters were sounded and the men retreated below deck, where they were locked up. Above, they could hear the bombs explode in the water near the ship. The Pope's gun crews quickly responded with the ship's anti-aircraft artillery, two five-inch cannons and several "pom-pom" guns.

Ketzler remembers the ship heeled nearly on its side as it zigzagged to avoid the bombs. He and his men stood helplessly by their bunks, with two canteens in hand and life jackets on.

The planes flew away, leaving the ship undamaged and no one hurt. Ketzler speculates that the planes probably were returning from another mission and were short on bombs and fuel. But Tokyo Rose didn't miss a beat. On-air, she told the men of the General Pope that they didn't have what they wanted this time, but Japanese submarines were laying in wait and would get them before they reached Bombay.

India

Bombay has a large shallow harbor with gates that open to allow ships to pass only during high tide. The General John Pope was a large ship and its propellers stirred up mud as it entered the harbor. It took three days to unload the men and supplies and Ketzler's group was one of the last off. They amused themselves watching the Air Corpsmen leave for Calcutta, and officers' footlockers being dropped on the dock and smashed. Just before they got off the ship, they received their back pay in Indian rupees. Ketzler kept the equivalent of 50 dollars and sent the rest home.

After three days a train pulled up next to the ship and Ketzler and his 53 charges boarded the train for Ledo, Assam in Northeast India. It would be a long trip, since Bombay is located on the central west coast of India. His men and a group of sergeants were being sent to replace soldiers in Burma.

The train was stark. Ketzler had a private compartment, but the men were in cars with long wooden benches up the middle. They couldn't sleep on the benches, so Ketzler had them tear them out to give them more space, and many of the men slept on the baggage racks. The latrines were two cement "feet" above a hole over the tracks. There was no communication between the cars except when the train stopped, which it did frequently. Their meals consisted of C-rations and powdered coffee. To heat water for the coffee, they got off at a stop and gave the engineer two annas – about four cents – to blow the whistle. They put their canteen cups over the whistle and got scalding water.

Along the way, Indian men would jump onto the train to sell goods to the soldiers. Ketzler ordered one man off, and when he didn't leave, threw him from the moving train. He thinks he might have hit one of the steel telephone poles that lined the track.

When another Indian man got on to sell a small monkey, the men asked Ketzler's permission to buy it. Ketzler told them no, that it would shit all over the train, but the men promised to take care of it. The man was only asking 10 dollars for the monkey, and the train ride would be long, so Ketzler decided it would be good for morale. But, he told the men, the first piece of crap he found – off goes the monkey. When the men asked what to use for the monkey's latrine, Ketzler suggested using their mess kits. They wouldn't need them on the train because they had food in tins and C-rations.

The men taught the monkey well. With 53 guys watching, every time it squatted someone produced a mess kit. Pretty soon, whenever the monkey needed to go, it would just bang on a mess kit. The men shared their C-rations with the monkey and bought it fruit at the numerous train stops, during which it proved to be a great attraction for the whole train.

They had to change trains three times on the trip to Ledo, each time to cross a major river. They walked three or four miles to reach the ferryboat and paid the Indians five rupees (about 15 cents) to carry their bags. Ketzler recalls that when the men decided five rupees wasn't enough and increased it to ten, a British soldier screamed at them for ruining the economy. On the other side of the river, they boarded another train. Each one was a narrower gauge as they got further into the jungle, so the quarters became increasingly cramped.

* * *

One of the soldiers, who had also been at Fort Riley, didn't get along with his sergeant, so Ketzler traded one of his men for him. The soldier, a Greek by the name of Pappas, was quite a good card player and had won a lot of money aboard ship. At the train stops, when Indian children would run up to the soldiers, begging, Pappas got them to stand in line. He would then dole out an anna to each child. The other soldiers chided him, saying that the children who received an anna would just run to the back of the line and get another handout. "Pappas, can't you see you're just throwing your money away," the men taunted. Pappas replied, "This isn't my money – I sent mine home. This is your money." Which, of course, made the other men furious. Pappas' sergeant wanted him to stop giving the children handouts and making the men angry, but Ketzler didn't see the harm in it.

Ketzler later saw Pappas after the battle of Myitkyina (Mitch'-en-ow) where he had been transferred to the 124th, the Texas Cavalry. The group flew the Texas flag, and charged seven hills in the battle. It also had a 60 percent casualty rate, and Pappas was one of them. It seemed the Greek didn't have a real tooth in his head – they were all false. When Pappas fell during the battle, the false teeth popped out and smashed on a rock. With nothing to eat but C-rations, a soldier couldn't survive without his teeth. Pappas was evacuated and sent home with a Purple Heart.

Ledo, Assam, India

Ledo is in the Assam province in Northeast India, near the border with Burma. It is in a low-lying area that receives a lot of rain and is surrounded by mountainous jungle. Communication and transportation are limited. The flat areas of Assam served as the airfields for planes flying Over the Hump to China or down to Myitkyina. Ledo served as an Army supply depot, transporting supplies to China and Burma. In Ledo they were outfitted for the things they would need for jungle duty.

When Ketzler was there it was rainy and muddy. The tropical jungle climate meant an abundance of mosquitoes, flies, spiders, scorpions, rats and snakes, many poisonous. In the morning, the men had to make sure there were no scorpions inside their boots before they put them on. They also had to be careful of where they put their hands or where they sat.

Ketzler, far right, in living quarters at Ledo

At the supply depot, the men were given the supplies they would need in Burma, but were also cautioned to take as little as possible, because they would have to carry everything. The men did everything they could to lighten their duffle bags. They pulled the top off their mess kits, but kept the bottoms, which could be used for frying. They were given a fork, spoon and knife, but kept only the spoon as they could use their bayonet as a knife. They had a canteen cup and two canteens. They cut their blanket and a towel in half. Some men even cut the sleeves off their fatigues. The men cleaned their mess kits by dipping them in soapy water, rinsing them with scalding water and hanging them on a rope to dry. But they couldn't break the monkey's habit of using the mess kits as a latrine. When a soldier wanted to have some fun, he would pick a mess kit off the line and bang it on the ground. The soldiers would all come running to get their mess kit before the monkey used it.

While in Ledo, the men continued rigorous training until they were assigned. Since men were badly needed in the battle to take Myitkyina, Ketzler's group was quickly assigned to join the 124th Cavalry. (This was the same 124th Cavalry that Ketzler was originally slated to join patrolling the U.S. – Mexican border after he finished basic training.) Although Ketzler was also assigned to the 124th Cavalry, the group of Texans didn't want any more sergeants. They wanted to promote their own, and they certainly didn't want a

Ketzler at the air strip in Lido waiting for transport into Burma

non-Texan. Ketzler twice almost boarded the plane, but both times saw his orders changed. Meanwhile, he had plenty of assignments in Ledo. He trained some Chinese troops as truck drivers and taught weapons to a group of Gurkhas from Nepal. It was the same job he had at Fort Riley, but these trainees couldn't speak English.

* * *

At one point, a group of Australian horses were flown in to Ledo to be used in the war effort. These horses were wild, right out of the outback. A request went out for anyone who knew about horses. Ketzler and several others from Fort Riley immediately volunteered. They were to take the horses from the planes to the depot about five miles from the airstrip. At one point they had to lead the horses across a narrow, temporary bridge that had no sides. It was about a 15-foot drop to the stream bed. The horses looked at one side and promptly shied away from the drop, only to fall off the other side. Ketzler had them lead the horses in pairs. Each horse backed away from its side, but into the other horse. They were so tight together, Ketzler said, that a dollar bill would stay put between them, but they made it across the stream.

When two soldiers who were out on patrol in the mountainous area around Ledo hadn't returned, Ketzler was one of six men who volunteered to go look for them. The area was mountainous, dense forest and there were no maps. They used a compass to go in the direction they thought the men had gone. They carried only minimal supplies, because an airplane from Ledo was scheduled to drop additional supplies after two days. The plane did come back in two days, but they only dropped a card telling Ketzler's group that the missing men had returned, and to come on back. There were no supplies. Ketzler and the men were left to forage for themselves. They cut bamboo to get water from the sections, cut hearts from the palm trees, and scavenged for whatever food they could eat raw. At one point they found a village, and bought and cooked a suckling pig. They finally found a river leading back to Ledo. During the night they walked in the river, but during the day they had to stay under the cover of the dense forest. Ketzler picked up a fungus from the river that still reappears every two or three years. After two weeks, Ketzler finally got an assignment to go to Myitkyina.

Myitkyina, Burma

When Ketzler arrived by plane, Japanese snipers were shooting at them from both the island in the river and from the town. It was the middle of the battle to take the city of Myitkyina. The battle had started about a month before and it would be another month before the Japanese were driven out.

Myitkyina had the largest hard surface airstrip in northern Burma. Japanese control of both the town and the airstrip for a number of years had effectively cut off overland supplies to China. It was also causing major obstacles to air supply. Japanese fighter planes based in Myitkyina constantly attacked planes flying Over the Hump from India into China. To avoid them, the Allied planes were forced to fly further north, over the Himalayas, at altitudes of over 20,000 feet. The weather was at best unpredictable and often made flying impossible. The Allies flying out of the Assam airfields were losing more 50 planes a month.

General "Vinegar Joe" Stilwell was trying to defeat the Japanese in Burma and open up the land supply routes to China, so Myitkyina became a major focus. Stilwell had trained and outfitted six Chinese divisions and was using them in Burma to drive the Japanese out. On May 17, 1944, Chinese troops and Merrill's Marauders made a surprise attack and took Myitkyina's airstrip. But taking the town wasn't as quick.

Myitkyina is a large city which was originally held by an estimated 350 Japanese troops. It is located on the Irrawaddy River whose ice-cold waters flow directly from the Himalayas to the Indian Ocean. Myitkyina's airstrip was built in the flood plain along the river. The town sits in the hills, overlooking the river, making the air strip an easy target for Japanese snipers. Taking the airstrip caused supply problems for the Japanese in the city, but it wasn't of much use to the Allied planes if they didn't also have the town. By the time Ketzler arrived, there were about 7,000 Japanese in the city who had come in through the thin Allied lines.

The battle had not gone well the first month. There were heavy Chinese casualties, so the Allies began sending more troops to the area to join in the fight. They also began intensive bombing of the city. General Stilwell ordered every man who could fire a rifle, including many of sick and walking wounded, to join in the effort.

Other Allied troops joined in, including the English, Irish, Welsh, Scots, Newfoundlanders, Australians, Canadians, New Zealanders, East Africans, South Africans, and the Chinese troops under General Stilwell. Also fighting were the native groups in Burma, including the Kachins, Shans, Chins, Karens, and Burmese. Many Indian groups were there including the Naga headhunters. From Nepal were the fierce Gurkhas. They said there were more nationalities in that battle than in any battle in WWII.

But many of the soldiers in the area were engineers who were there building the Ledo road. They could bridge the largest rivers and move the highest mountains, but they had little combat or weapons experience and carried only machetes.

Ketzler was not specifically assigned to any one unit but his experience as a drill sergeant was quickly put to use. His first job was to train a group of 12 engineers to load and fire weapons. Since there were no weapons available to these men, Ketzler went down to the hospital. (actually just an area where the wounded were put on blankets waiting to be evacuated) and found stacks of weapons no longer needed by the wounded. Some were good and others were in disrepair. He used the parts of the broken weapons to make working weapons. Once the first group was trained, the men were put on the lines and he was given another group.

Ledo Road, Burma, near Myitkyina 1944

Battle of Myitkyina 1943

The Battle of Myitkyina has been described as some of the worst fighting in WWII. It was early summer, nearing the end of the monsoon season, so the whole valley was a sea of mud. The weather was unbearably hot and muggy and rained every day. The men slept on their half blankets on the ground without the benefit of tents or mosquito nets. Ketzler remembers eating beans out of a tin can, watching the water drip off his helmet into the can. They fought diseases like cholera, smallpox, malaria and dysentery, as well as jungle insects, snakes and wild animals. Day after day, they were forced to stay in foxholes and slit trenches flooded with water up to their chests. Enemy snipers kept the men pinned down most of the time. When he wasn't training men, Ketzler slipped from group to group, helping site weapons.

The enemy was very near, but often hard to see or recognize. Ketzler remembers it was especially terrifying at night when it was pitch dark. The Japanese could be dug in just a few feet away. If a grenade was thrown, it was sometimes rolled right back by the enemy. When the Japanese killed a Chinese soldier they would take his uniform. Then, disguised as Chinese, they would turn around and kill Americans. To prevent that, the Americans issued pieces of colored cloth to the Chinese. The color was changed every day and the Chinese and Allies knew the color. If the Chinese soldier was wearing the wrong color for that day – he would probably be shot.

Photo of two Japanese soldiers found on the ground of an abandoned Japanese camp near Myitkyina, 1943

The intense bombing raids and increased Allied troop strength finally paid off. The town of Myitkyina fell on August 3. Most of the Japanese escaped by floating down the river on rafts. The Japanese general, who had been told to fight to the last man, committed hari-kari. The only Japanese captured were those on the island in the Irrawaddy River. To convince them to surrender, the Americans used Nisei, American soldiers of Japanese descent, who could speak both languages. Nisei were incidentals used to communicate with the Japanese, and were in a very dangerous position in wartime. But they convinced the Japanese on the island to surrender.

* * *

49

Pontoon bridge across the Irrawaddy River, Myitkyina, 1944

As soon as the battle ended and the Japanese left, the Americans built a pontoon bridge across the Irrawaddy so the trucks could be driven across rather than be ferried. It was the largest pontoon bridge in the world. The building of the Ledo Road continued but there was still another 80 miles to go before it reached Myitkyina. The Allied forces reorganized to push the Japanese to the south and continued building the road. Mules were brought into Myitkyina by plane to support the effort. Ketzler never actually got into the town. Since he knew horses he was immediately sent down to the 155th quartermaster company, a mule pack outfit.

They organized the 124th, 475th, 912th and 913th artillery outfits, another mule pack, and the 50th and 22nd Chinese divisions. These were the troops that had taken Myitkyina. Now their mission was to go south to Bhamo, and on to Lashio.

Ketzler's assignment was a platoon of mule-packers supporting the 50th Chinese Division and the 124th (Texas) Cavalry. They stayed about five miles behind the lines. Supplies were air dropped and they would pick them up and take them down to the troops. The planes flew in low – about 500 feet – using the protection of the dense forest to avoid being shot at from the ground. The parachutes opened close to the ground so the supplies hit hard. They tried air dropping without parachutes, but Ketzler remembered there were beans all over the field. They also dropped water and grain for the mules.

Planes flew low over trees to escape ground fire while dropping supplies

Ketzler was with the 155th that Christmas, but it was just another day in a war zone. He was assigned guard duty once a week and that year his guard duty fell on Christmas Eve, New Year's Eve and his birthday, January 7.

Tigers, snakes, jungle birds and other animals were numerous, but Ketzler mostly remembers the monkeys. The trees were about 300 feet high and created three canopies. There were hundreds of monkeys in the top canopy. As soldiers moved, the monkeys chattered like mad, but if the soldiers stopped, there was suddenly dead silence. Once they started to move, the monkeys would again start their chatter.

Mule pack trains on the Ledo Road

They kept moving south but progress was slow. After three weeks, they had traveled just a short distance when the order came to pull out two divisions of Chinese.

At that time the Japanese were causing major problems in China. They had taken the port cities of Nanking, Shanghai and Kweilin, an airstrip that gave their planes easy access to the South China coast. But although they held the cities, if they ventured a mile outside the cities, they risked being shot by the Chinese. In retaliation, the Japanese initiated a brutal scorched earth policy, burning the villages and slaughtering the people.

General Stilwell had trained and outfitted six divisions of Chinese who were fighting in Burma. Chiang Kai-shek wanted them back to help fight the Japanese in China. Stilwell talked Chiang into taking just two divisions and said he would send some of the American troops with them.

Ketzler was "some of the American troops."

Driving The Ledo Road – Myitkyina to Ledo

The two divisions of Chinese, along with Ketzler retuned to Myitkyina where most of the Chinese were flown to China. Ketzler's assignment was to take three trucks with supplies and 22 non-English-speaking Chinese soldiers up the Ledo Road; they would fly to China from Ledo.

Studebaker truck with mounted weapons

The Ledo Road was still under construction, but nearly completed between Myitkyina and Ledo. There were very few towns along the way, mostly just Army engineering camps where they could stop for gasoline and rations. There was little traffic and the road twisted and turned through the dense jungle, over rivers, across swamps and over steep, mountain passes. Most of the way was slow going and muddy. The Chinese rode on top of the trucks and there were two Chinese in the cabs, including the drivers.

At the end of the first day, the lead truck in which Ketzler was riding developed engine trouble. The Chinese driver said the equivalent of "no problem" and suddenly turned off the main road onto a narrow jungle path. Ketzler, alarmed, ordered him to stop the truck. The driver tried to tell him not to worry, but Ketzler saw himself, one white soldier, alone in the jungle with three trucks loaded with supplies and 22 Chinese. It would be nothing for them to kill Ketzler, and take the three trucks and supplies. He drew his pistol and put it to the driver's head, again ordering him to stop. But the driver insisted they continue. In less than a mile, they came to a clearing. Ketzler still had his pistol to the driver's head when he realized they had entered some kind of maintenance station manned by Chinese, supervised by American soldiers.

An American solder came out to greet them and assured Ketzler the truck could be fixed by morning. He invited him into the mess for dinner and offered a place to sleep. The Chinese soldiers had their own mess so his Chinese troops joined them. In the morning the truck was fixed and they were on their way. It had turned out fine, Ketzler said, but "that incident really scared the shit out of me."

"Chinese Bandits" in Chinese army uniforms were one of the hazards of the Ledo road. At that time Blacks were not allowed in China and a group of Chinese soldiers had attacked and killed a whole convoy of black soldiers. As a result, the black soldiers were very leery of the Chinese. Most of the trucks were black units with white officers and it was not unusual for them to run Chinese driven trucks off the road. To protect his convoy, Ketzler rode in the front and every time he saw a truck coming toward them, he got out, hollered and waved to let them know he was with them.

While on the road, Ketzler heard that two black soldiers had "gone native." They lived in the jungle along the road. Blacks passing through the area in trucks would kick off rations for them. The AWOL black solders had a lot of status with the native people. They would go into a little village and become the headman because they could supply all kinds of rations.

At times the trucks could only make about 2.5 mph in mud that was up to the hubs. With six low gears, they didn't get stuck but they moved very slowly. Most of the trucks were American Jimmies and Studebakers. The Studebakers had doors on them so the first thing the soldiers did was remove the doors: Every once in a while a truck would go off the side and roll down the hill, and the soldiers wanted to make sure they could jump out.

It was 268 miles from Myitkyina to Ledo on the road and the trip took four days. By the end of the second day they got to Shingbwiyang (Shin'-a-wang), 103 miles from Ledo. From there on the terrain was mountainous. They started from Shingbwiyang at first light and drove hard all day. Chinglow Hill, about five miles from Shingbwiyang, consisted of seven miles of steep grades, sharp curves, and long switchbacks. That night, from high above on the mountain, they were still looking at the lights of Shingbwiyang.

Pangsau Pass is at mile 36 from Ledo where the road crosses the China-Burma Border near its highest point at about 4,600 feet. Here Ketzler encountered a major traffic jam. They had to wait in line for a monstrous bulldozer, which would hook onto their trucks one at a time, to keep them from sliding down the almost vertical drop. When the bulldozer got to the bottom, it hooked onto another truck and pulled it up. It was a slow process, but it was the only way to get over that area.

Pangsau Pass is a part of the Naga Hills, which runs along the Burma – India border. The hills are named *Kachin Unit, Burma 1944* after the tribe of headhunters who live there. The area had lot of good trails, well maintained and wide enough for a jeep, built by the Nagas under supervision of the British army. As the story goes, the Nagas from one village would get drunk and chop off a few heads and steal the women of a neighboring village. The British, using Gurkhas, captured and burned the aggressor village and put its people to the task of clearing trails. After six month's work, or whatever the penalty was, the British would let them go back to rebuild their village. The villages only had 20-30 people. It consisted of a large hut, or bashi, for the extended ruling family and small bashis for the other families. Ketzler remembers that if you had to get out and walk, the trails in the Naga Hills were pretty good.

Packing along Ledo Road

Naga Tribes, Burma

After four days on the road Ketzler says, "We got to Ledo with the three trucks and 22 Chinese, but I don't think they were same Chinese I started with."

Some of the Chinese divisions went up to the Salween River, on the border between China and Burma to repair a bridge that had been blown up. Although Ketzler didn't go, he was told that it was that spectacularly beautiful, that the Grand Canyon looked like an irrigation ditch compared to that valley.

Once in Ledo, they turned in the trucks and Ketzler could finally write his folks. It had been a long time, and they had actually had the Red Cross track him down in Myitkyina because they hadn't heard from him in months. Maintaining correspondence was difficult. Letters had to go through Army censors and the officers had better things to do than play postal censor in the middle of the conflict.

When his folks heard he was in Ledo they contacted family acquaintances, the Landons, parents of Mickey Landon, who then managed to find Ketzler. Landon was a crew chief with the Air Corp, flying on C-47s out of Ledo and Over the Hump. He came over to Ketzler's camp to look him up and invited him over to the Air Corps quarters for a steak dinner. Afterwards they dropped in at the Air Corps club. Ketzler thought the Air Corps had it great. They returned every night to a steak dinner and a nice evening, while the Cavalry, just across town, dined on meals poured out of tin cans by the "walking wounded."

China

By Dec. 1, 1944, the Japanese offensive in Southern China had destroyed U.S. airfields in Hunan and Kwangsi. Chinese troops and U.S. aircraft had to be moved to protect Kunming and Chunking. Convoys on the Burma Road from Wan-king to Kunming were resumed on Jan. 18, 1945.

Ketzler and his Chinese troops landed at the airstrip at Kunming and from there took trucks down to Kweilin, walking much of the way. Kweilin was an airstrip with easy access to the China Sea which had been taken by the Japanese because the Allied Forces were using it to attack Japanese ships. When Ketzler arrived the Allied forces were in the process of retaking Kweilin using full force. His role was supervising fighting troops.

The Chinese were helping fight the Japanese, but they were also engaged in a civil war. Chiang Kai-shek threatened to surrender to the Japanese if the U.S. didn't send him more troops and supplies. He didn't want to use any of his troops because Mao Tse Tung was up north with the Chinese Communist troops, ready to overtake the Kuomintang (Chinese Nationals). The Americans wanted the communists to get into the fight with the Japanese, but Chiang objected to our training the Communist Chinese because they could then fight against the Nationals in the civil war.

* * *

In Kweilin, Ketzler's Chinese troops were melded into a division of about 2,500. In his opinion, the Kuomintang officer corps was not good: the Chinese officers were so corrupt that they were actually taking weapons that the U.S. had flown into China and selling them to the Japanese, who then used them against the Allied forces. The military officers and the Nationalists, except for the common soldier, held all the money, which they basically stole from their own men. Although the common soldier was paid about 8 dollars a month, it was first sent to the generals, who skimmed some off the top before sending the rest down to the colonels. The Colonels then siphoned off some of it, then sent it down to the majors. The majors also skimmed some off. By the time the soldier received his pay, it amounted to about 80 cents, Ketzler said.

"Chiang Kai-shek's whole system was corrupt from the top down. The rank and file Chinese knew it. But they were peasants and weren't educated. They believed you were born, you live until you die, and you just get along. The Communists told the peasants that was wrong and they were going to fix it. They had a cause. The Kuomintang didn't have a cause, other than the rich getting richer and the poor getting poorer.

"When I got back to the United States I told people that Communism isn't for me, and I am not suggesting it for the U.S., but in a country that is so badly corrupt, it seemed to be a good thing. It was brutal. If you were corrupt, the Communists shot you. If you were terminally ill, they shot you. There was no corruption, because they didn't tolerate it: you didn't throw a piece of paper on the ground. They told the people what to do and they enforced it. When you have two billion uneducated people, that's the only way you can control them. I wasn't all that popular when I got back and suggested Communism might be the best thing for the Chinese. It was the era where we were fighting communism, the terrible curse."

Once in China, Ketzler had a fanji won (Interpreter) Frederick Chiang, assigned to him. Chiang was with him constantly. He was intelligent and his father was in charge of all railroads in Southern China. Ketzler had learned some Chinese, but nothing technical. He could get along, but needed an interpreter for all else.

At mealtime, Ketzler and the 14 other Americans were given two bowls, which they took through the line to two big tubs. The water off the rice was used for soup or tea. Grass was added to the top of the rice. That was the greens. It was a bit monotonous, but they survived on it. Life improved immensely once Ketzler got to Kunming.

He flew from Kweilin on a C46 (Equivalent to a civilian DC3). Most of the planes didn't have doors and weren't pressurized so everyone had to wear oxygen masks. Ketzler remembers that his friend Whitey Powell scoffed at the oxygen masks, saying he didn't smell anything so it must not be doing any good. He left it and went back to the can. Pretty soon the door opened and he came out, crawling on his hands and knees. Ketzler and the others went back and grabbed him and put the oxygen mask on him. "You dumb dodo ….you can't smell oxygen," Ketzler scolded.

Kunming

Kunming, in southwestern China, lies in a broad scenic valley with a very large lake. It has lush vegetation, a lot of sunshine and is reputed to have the best climate in China. In the distance one can see the sharp mountains of the Himalayas.

When Ketzler arrived, Kunming was a small town, about the size of Fremont, Nebraska. But with the Japanese threatening that area, more and more Chinese came into Kunming from the surrounding areas seeking protection. Its population rapidly swelled to about 100,000. The native Chinese, mostly Miao, Yi, and Hans came in and established quarters wherever they could. Some had nothing but mud huts on a small plot of land just outside the walls of Kunming where they grew some vegetables. Ketzler remembers them as beautiful people.

"When Bets and I went back in 1995, Kunming had about a million and a half people. It is a modern city and the Capital of Yunan province with a major university. I couldn't find one thing that was the same."

Two of the many gates at Kunming

China 1944

Kunming 1944

The first night Ketzler arrived in Kunming he decided to take a walk up in the hills surrounding the city. He was on a mountainous ox cart trail when he rounded a bend and discovered a Chinese temple in the middle of nowhere. It was beautiful, with three sides and an open front. There were large, life-size statues of men with some unusual features. One had a very long pointing arm, another, a grotesque head, and all beautifully painted.

Ketzler noticed that there were cots in the temple, apparently quarters for a group of Chinese National soldiers. One soldier approached and since Ketzler had learned a little Chinese by this time, they talked. The Chinese soldier called out to one of the others and gave him an order. The man left and quickly returned with a large jar of rice wine. The soldier said, "Yi, ur, san, gon bay." (One, two, three, down the hatch.) The two of them enjoyed the wine and conversation the rest of the day.

Waking up in the U.S. tent camp the next morning, Ketzler wondered where he was. The others told him he had been carried in the night before, passed out in the arms of a Chinese Nationalist soldier. "I could have been killed up there and no one would have ever found me," Ketzler said.

Kunming was a major base for the Chinese Nationalist Army and the home of a training school for field grade officers, Major and above. Ketzler was to continue doing the job he did best, weapons training. He gave instructions on American and British weapons to the officers, who were to take that knowledge back to train their units. Ketzler's specialties included 81 mm and 60 mm mortars,

Ketzler and a Chinese soldier in the hills outside Kunming, 1944

anti-tank weapons, 37 mm cannons and bazookas. He also taught them to use a Bouys anti-tank rifle, which was a .55-caliber shoulder weapon.

During training, Ketzler instructed the Chinese officers to fire two rounds, holding the gun tightly against the shoulder to minimize the kickback, which on a .55-caliber is pretty hard. When the officers fired their first round and felt the kickback, they let out a yell. And when they fired the second round, they held it further away from their shoulder, which of course meant that the kickback was even more powerful.

* * *

Living conditions were much improved at the Officers Training School, located at Hostile 8, just outside Kunming. They enjoyed European style food prepared by excellent chefs. Their quarters were in comfortable tents with cement floors 4-foot cement sides. The weather was also a big improvement over the jungle.

Nearby was an airplane factory where they made airplanes much the way children make toy planes, by wetting the wood, bending it and then covering it with fabric.

The school decided it would relocate at Hostile 10, an old dilapidated Chinese fort about 10 miles from Hostile 8. Six of the Americans, including Ketzler, were sent there to supervise the Fort's renovation. He remembers that, in that short distance from Hostile 8, the dialect was entirely different and they had to learn to speak some Chinese all over again.

The fort was in extremely bad condition when they arrived. Huge rats were everywhere and the men said they would rather make camp outside its walls. They built cement slabs and 4-foot walls for their tents. They had to do their own messing and were given a 12-pound tin of "Bully Beef" (Canned Mutton from Australia), a bag of flour, and a tin of sausage for the four-weeks construction period. They could go into a nearby village to get vegetables and an occasional egg, but basically had Bully Beef and Sausage cooked in every way possible.

Ketzler hired a group of Chinese coolies as carpenters. He had one crew filling the rat holes, putting lime and clay in the holes so the rats wouldn't dig out. It didn't work. "We would sit around the table playing cards at night. I would pull out my pistol and, with my left arm, move a guy's head aside so I could shoot a rat. We killed a lot of rats."

There were dead rats in the water from the well so they had to boil it and add halazone tablets. It was common to have diarrhea in China. The Chinese all had it because the sanitation facilities were so bad. Their toilets consisted of just a pit laid over with about a 4" diameter log on which to sit. Every morning guys would come and dip it out and put it into the "honey buckets" destined for the vegetable fields.

One day an American soldier, new to China, was assigned to the construction project. After about three days, he asked to speak to Ketzler – privately, where he confided to Ketzler that he had fleas. Ketzler just laughed. "Everyone has fleas," he said.

* * *

The Chinese carpenters building bunk beds for the new school's barracks arrived every morning. Ketzler instructed them to continue making bunk beds and carefully counted out the 32 nails the Chinese said they needed to make two bunk beds. Nails were very valuable on the black market, so they had to be watched carefully. At night Ketzler inspected the newly constructed beds and counted the nails. After about a week, he discovered that the Chinese carpenters were cutting the nails into about ten little pieces. They were able to fit the wood together so perfectly that the bunk beds would be supported without any nails. They pounded in the little pieces so that when Ketzler counted the nails, it appeared they were all used. The Chinese were selling the nails on the black market for between 50 cents to one dollar each. Ketzler felt he was being cheated and told them after this they had to use the whole nails.

When work on the old fort was finished, the school moved to Hostile 10 where it remained until the war was over. The school had about 60 enlisted men and about 10 officers and, under an agreement with Chiang Kai-shek, the American soldiers would train Nationalist soldiers.

Just 500 yards from Ketzler's camp was a compound with

about 30,000 Communist soldiers. They were state troops who supported the Yunan Province, and were run by a War Lord who gained his riches by taxing. Ketzler remembers the Communists were very good soldiers. They would stay at their wall and watch the Americans teaching the Nationalist Chinese in weapons instruction. The Americans got word from Intelligence that, on August 20, the Communists were planning to take over the camp, capture everyone and take the planes.

Ketzler in Kunming

The Americans decided to stage "a magic five minutes," a great display of power. They took machine gun belts with every fifth round a tracer and replaced all the rounds with tracers, which were easily seen. They lined up machine gun after machine gun. They fired the bazookas, the .50-calibers and the mortars. They fired essentially everything they had.

"In five minutes we put on the damnedest exhibition of firepower you have ever seen. You could have walked across the tracers. The wall was full of these guys watching. We wanted them to know that if they tried to take us, it wasn't going to be easy," said Ketzler.

* * *

In China the dead are buried at ground level, covered by a mound. During a weapons demonstration Ketzler's trainees were firing bazookas, which have an inertia type firing pin; once the rocket is fired, it doesn't actually explode until it hits something. Several of the bazooka rounds hit grave mounds, then glanced off and slid through the grass to a stop. They didn't explode, which meant there were some live bazooka rounds out in the field. When the demonstration was finished, the communists would run into the field to pick up whatever was left. They once took a bazooka shell back to their compound and dropped it. It exploded and killed 18 of them, which caused a diplomatic problem as the Chinese thought it had been fired into their compound.

Toward the end of the war, the Communists came in from the hills. Things were getting bad. The Japanese were in bad shape because they couldn't get supplies and they were falling back further and further into China. Ketzler's crew got intelligence reports that the Communists who were in this neighboring compound were going to attack and take the airstrip, the depot and supplies in Kunming.

Ketzler and his men were ordered to stay and defend the airstrip to the last man. The Air Corps wanted to get their planes and supplies out and Ketzler's troop was told to hold off the enemy until help arrived. But no help was coming. "It was a suicide mission," Ketzler said. Before the action started, "I, like most of the other guys in the group, all got a nap sack . . . I got ammunition, socks, and canteens of water – to go over the hill if they started something. Fortunately, it didn't ever come about because the Communists found out that the Japanese were quitting and the Americans were prepared to fight."

At the Kunming training school Ketzler at times became frustrated with the Chinese – they weren't very serious about fighting. It wasn't really their war and they really were not soldiers. At one point, the Colonel called Ketzler on the carpet for yelling at the Chinese. He told Ketzler that their mission was just to keep the Chinese in the war. He shouldn't worry if they weren't good students, and he definitely shouldn't yell at them. He urged Ketzler not to get frustrated. But that was often easier said than done. One field exercise with the 81 mm mortar illustrated that point.

Firing an 81 mm mortar required two men; one sited the gun and the other one loaded it. On this particular day, the two soldiers had an aiming stake and two targets, which were located on a high hill with no trees. Below the two was a group of Chinese working in the rice paddies. One soldier sited in on the target. Ketzler checked it, gave the OK to fire, and then went over to check the other tube. When Ketzler glanced back over at the first soldier, he saw that the man had resited the tube. It was now aiming directly at the Chinese in the rice paddy. Before Ketzler could stop him, the soldier fired the round. Since a mortar goes way up, and then comes down, the Chinese below heard it incoming and lay down. The round fell right in the middle of the rice paddies. "I screamed at them, but they were all laughing," Ketzler said. "It was a big joke. Life is so meaningless to them."

* * *

The Allied declared Victory in Europe while Ketzler was in Kunming. Many of the planes, which had been in Europe, now flew into Kunming. "It was getting really heavy for the Japs because of the extra planes. We were very excited about the Victory in Europe, but we were still in the war. Now we were going to finish it," Ketzler said.

The Rodeo at Kunming

With the war over in Europe, the Red Cross and USO focused their attention on China, which before had largely been ignored. They came to Kunming and asked what the men wanted for entertainment. Since the Americans there were largely Horse Cavalrymen, Westerners and horse people, they suggested that a Rodeo would be great fun. The USO worked hard to make it happen.

There were some mules at the 20th General and a remount station at L-12, which was 12 miles out of Ledo and about 250 miles from Kunming by land. The USO went on the open market and bought a bunch of Brahma steers in Ledo. For 50 days, they marched the mules and Brahma steers on the road to Kunming.

Meanwhile, many of the men stationed in Kunming sent home for Western hats. By the time of the rodeo, everyone was wearing a Western hat and walking bow-legged. They even had a rodeo queen. The whole camp turned into a Western Las Vegas-type resort. It was time to celebrate and they were going to have a rodeo.

High-level officers and other officials from Kunming, generals and Air Corps were all invited. A few days before the rodeo, they found out that the steers and the mules were still about three day's away. So they ran the mules and the Brahma steers the rest of the way, arriving at Kunming the night before the rodeo. The animals were exhausted. It had also been pouring rain for three days. By the time of the rodeo, the grounds were in a foot of mud soup.

The Brahma steers were so inbred, they were about the size of a Shetland pony, and made for a hilarious sight. When a cowboy mounted one of the diminutive steers, his boots dragged on the ground through the mud.

A cowboy from Montana bragged that he was a great bronc rider and was going to ride a bucking mule. They shot the mule with juice, and it bucked inside the shoot until it flipped over with the cowboy from Montana lying underneath. Men on one side of the chute tried to pull him out one side, while the men on the other side of the chute tried to pull him the other way. Above the roar of the crowd, the guy, yelled "Would somebody please open this gate and let one of us dumb son' of a bitches out of here." So they opened the gate and let out first the mule, then got the man. In the Cavalry, the animals were always taken care of first.

Whitey Powell was the rodeo clown. He started at one end of the arena on a little mule and fell off in the mud. He had hold of the rope and the mule took off at a dead run. It was like a motorboat, with Whitey throwing up mud on both sides in a wake.

"That rodeo was the most disastrous thing I ever saw in my life." Ketzler said. "Recently there was a very short letter in the Ex-CBI Roundup. (They are encouraging people to write memories.) One man wrote that he remembered a Rodeo in Kunming. They had checked out a jeep to go see the rodeo and got caught in a foxhole. (I know it was a mud hole.) They walked over to see the rodeo and wondered if anyone else remembered it."

* * *

The war was winding down, and Ketzler was ordered to parachute into Japan with some Chinese troops to disrupt communications and generally cause problems. The invasion of Japan was planned, and the idea was that Ketzler and his Chinese troops would soon be rescued by invading Allied forces.

Ketzler saw it differently. The Chinese troops could put on Japanese clothes and disappear into the landscape – but he was obviously a Caucasian. And if that didn't scare him, jumping out of a plane certainly did. Ketzler wanted no part of it. He shared the mess hall with a group of paratroopers who told him he had to practice jumping – but not to worry. They also reassured him that they would shove him out the door of the plane, all he had to do was pull the cord. And if the first shoot didn't open, he could pull the second cord. Ketzler didn't like the idea at all. Luckily, he was saved by the bomb.

Japan Surrenders But Chinese Officers' School Continues

On Aug. 6, 1945, it came over the wire that America had dropped a nuclear bomb on Hiroshima. On August 9 another was dropped on Nagasaki. On August 10 the Japanese surrendered. (The formal surrender was September 2).

"We were all elated, firing weapons up into the air and celebrating. We all went down to Joe's Vodka and started drinking. I drank a lot of Joe's Vodka during that time. You took your bottle and he would open the spigot and fill it … so it was not aged . . . that well. It was hilarious," Ketzler said. But the Americans at Kunming celebrated alone. "The Chinese weren't all that mixed up in the war," he said, "so they didn't feel the impact of the surrender like we did." Even though the war with Japan was officially over, at the school at Kunming it was business as usual.

One day they were demonstrating weapons to 22 Chinese Generals. They discussed the weapon, its use and potential effects, and then fired it. Ketzler set up a rifle grenade demonstration in which blank cartridges were to be used to propel the grenade some 100 yards out, where it would safely explode.

Just then a jeep sped up to the demonstration site and slid to a stop. The driver yelled at Ketzler to get in immediately. Although he was just about to demonstrate the weapon, the driver told Ketzler to drop everything in order to catch a plane in 30 minutes. The driver took him back to his tent in order for him to grab his gear. While there, another jeep carrying a litter drove up. It was Whitey Powell. He had fired Ketzler's weapon, which malfunctioned. The grenade exploded on the end of the rifle. It didn't kill him, but he was badly injured. Later Ketzler saw him in Shanghai - He was fine, but he had some scars on his face. It was a sobering experience. "It could have been me," Ketzler said.

* * *

When Ketzler arrived at the airport, he found the plane waiting with engines running. A group of men stood beside the plane, and a lieutenant, who had obviously been drinking. The pilot yelled at Ketzler that these were now his men and to get them on the plane quickly. There were 35 men, more than they had seats, but Ketzler got them on board and strapped in. He asked the men who was in charge of the group, but no one seemed to know. "Surely someone has some rank," he said. "Where did you guys come from?"

Finally, one man said they had just come over the road from Ledo and the MPs were in charge. Totally confused, Ketzler asked, "What MPs?" The man replied that they were the same MPs who had brought the group from the U.S.

Now Ketzler understood. These men had all been in prison and had been paroled to go to combat zones. They were now under Ketzler's command.

When he asked if they had any weapons, they just laughed. "Who would give us weapons?" Ketzler spent some time talking to the men about their backgrounds and why they were in prison, and then selected two of the men to be acting sergeants, each over half the group.

The first man was an Arizonan named Sealy, who had been in prison for manslaughter. Sealy had gotten into a fight over a woman in a small, dusty town where they had a middle of the street shootout and he killed the guy. Ketzler put him in charge of the first section.

The other acting sergeant was a man named Beebe, from Ft. Dodge Iowa. He had stolen a bunch of tires and had some ROTC training. Ketzler put him in charge of the second section.

When they arrived in Kweilin, they were told to get off the plane fast and board another, larger plane, a C-54, which was waiting for them. As they scrambled aboard, Ketzler asked the pilot where they were going. "Shanghai," he said.

Sampans at Soo Chow Creek, Shanghaii

Shanghai

On Aug. 13, 1945, just three days after the Japanese verbally surrendered, Ketzler's plane approached Shanghai. The war was over, but the treaty hadn't been signed. The Japanese had controlled Shanghai and Ketzler wasn't sure they knew the war was over.

The pilot of the C-54 didn't think the Japanese at Shanghai were still at war, but he was taking no chances. When they approached the city, he circled until just before dark. When he landed, it was completely dark. The pilot told the men to jump off the plane as fast as possible. Minutes after they landed, he took off, disappearing in the total darkness. Ketzler, the lieutenant and the 35 prison parolees stood in the dark on the runway. Their only weapons were Ketzler's .45-caliber pistol and carbine, and the lieutenant's carbine.

Three trucks came out of the darkness. They were run by coal, which burned to make steam to run the engines, and were driven by old Japanese men. The oldest spoke some English, and told them to climb aboard. As it turned out, the Americans weren't the first into Shanghai. The Chinese were already there, setting up a base of operations. They had sent the trucks to pick up Ketzler's group. They were taken to temporary quarters in the Park Hotel, which was very nice, but the rooms were empty. The Japanese had taken all the furnishings.

The next morning, Ketzler looked out his window and saw he was directly above the horse stable. He went down and talked to the Japanese who were caring for the horses and equipment. All the Japanese officers had left, so Ketzler suggested they wouldn't need their saddles anymore. The Japanese told Van to help himself, and he took a nice forward seat saddle, which he still owns to this day. When he returned to Omaha, he rode it in the foxhunt for a few years. It was small, only 16 inches, and Ketzler usually rides an 18-

inch saddle, so fellow fox hunters would tell him it looked as if he was riding bareback.

In Shanghai, as the first order of business, Ketzler hired an interpreter, an Austrian Jew who had escaped to China during the war. He had no passport but was brilliant and spoke seven languages. Ketzler also hired a group of White Russians whose parents had escaped Russia during the World War I. They could speak Russian, Chinese and English. None of them had passports, either, so they had to stay in China.

After the first three or four days, Ketzler and his men moved to permanent quarters at the Grosner House, on Jaffrey Rue, a main street of Shanghai leading down to the Bund. The Bund ran along the river and was a Shanghai landmark before the war. It was on the edge of the international area, which had beautiful French, German, British, and American buildings, which were banks and embassies. The Bund was a very busy street, about 8-10 lanes wide.

Shanghai is at the mouth of the Yang Tze River, and has a deep harbor. At night it held a damp, penetrating cold. To keep warm, Ketzler would buy hot roasted chestnuts and have them poured them into the gauntlets of his gloves. When they cooled, he ate them.

When Ketzler arrived, the harbor was filled with large ships loaded with trucks and fuel for the anticipated invasion of Japan. Now that Japan had surrendered, the ships were being brought back to the docks and unloaded. Ketzler and his men arrived in Shanghai with only what they could carry, but now, every truck unloaded from the ships was assigned to him. Within a few weeks he had a motor pool and a fleet of more than 300 trucks. The warehouse district around the docks was called the Go Down and it is where they spent much of their time. Soon Ketzler had enough trucks and men to run 35 serials, each consisting of one American, one Russian who could speak Chinese and English, and three Chinese. That made about 175 men, each with a truck. Another 20-30 trucks were replacements when trucks were brought in for repair or service. A crew of about 20 White Russians and Chinese served as mechanics and kept the trucks running.

Ships being unloaded in Shanghai Harbor. They were loaded with fuel for the planned invasion of Japan. The Japanese surrender put an end to the war.

The primary goal was to get the gasoline off the ships and transport it to Shanghai's five airports. They transported the gas in 55-gallon drums, and each truck could carry 18 drums. A dispatcher kept track of where all the trucks were at any one time. The trucks would go to the Go Down district and the docks, load up and then take the gas wherever it was needed. Ketzler and his Austrian interpreter were well organized and in constant motion, checking on things from their jeep.

Chinese Wedding Parade in Shangaii

A large cement area surrounded by a fence provided an ideal place to park the trucks overnight. At first, Ketzler and his men worked long hours to get the operation up and running smoothly. At night, they filled all the gas tanks in order to be ready for morning, then returned to their quarters for a midnight dinner. A Chinese platoon was put in charge of guarding the compound overnight. When Ketzler and his men returned at 5 a.m., the trucks wouldn't start. They were out of gas. The Chinese guards were actually helping other Chinese to steal the gas. They could sell it on the black market for about 5 dollars a gallon.

Ketzler went down to the POW prison and asked for a squad of Japanese sailors and a chief petty officer. The guards flatly refused, but Ketzler went to his lieutenant and explained that he had to have the Japanese. Oh, and they also needed weapons.

The next day, a squad of Japanese sailors arrived under the supervision of a Japanese chief petty officer who was about the same age as Ketzler. They saluted smartly and lined up for inspection.

Street vendor rolling cigarettes in Shanghai

At first, Ketzler remembered sheepishly, he was pretty hard on them, holding constant inspections and finding fault with the slightest thing. But the Japanese performed well and obeyed. Their chief would clap his hands and one of the sailors would break away and come back with tea and sake, which Ketzler and the chief enjoyed together.

Ketzler remembers that on the first night the Japanese sailors stood guard over the compound, it sounded like the 4th of July. The Japanese sailors were shooting at the Chinese who came in to steal the gas. From that day on, they never lost another gallon of gas. Soon Ketzler's inspections were much more relaxed and his friendship with the chief petty officer grew. He could speak some English, so the two enjoyed talking. One morning he brought out some Japanese war maps to share with Ketzler. They were written in Japanese, but he translated and pointed out on the map where noted American ships had been sunk. Ketzler noticed there were three different locations for the sinking of the same American aircraft carrier. Ketzler pointed out the error. The chief didn't bring out the maps again.

After about three weeks, Ketzler came over to have his customary glass of hot tea and sake. The chief showed him where he had dug a hole and buried two Japanese Samurai sabers, a Japanese flag which had flown over the headquarters, and a couple of other pieces of gear. He gave them to Ketzler as a gesture of friendship. Ketzler's son Jon has one of the swords and the flag. Ketzler gave the other sword to his Uncle Ken.

Young Japanese Petty Officer Ketzler came to trust

Their operation was now running smoothly and Ketzler and his men could cut back their hours to about 10 hours a day. They had a little more free time in Shanghai. Many of the beautiful buildings were still standing because during the war with the U.S., the Japanese cleared out the top two floors of every building and housed women and children civilians there. The U.S. planners knew that the top of almost every building had civilians in it so they didn't bomb those buildings. The Americans were primarily targeting ships and the Go Downs.

Their hotel was in a beautiful part of the city called French Town. It was in a compound facing Jaffrey Rue with a big garden on one side. Across the garden was Cathay Mansion where the officers lived. There were two 3-bedroom apartments on each floor with an elevator between them. Ketzler and his men had apartments on the third and fourth floors. There was no furniture, so they brought in cots and other items. But each apartment did have plumbing and a bath so they were very comfortable. They sometimes brought home "10 in One" rations (one tin served ten people) which they took from ships being unloaded.

A Chinese houseboy did their cooking, cleaning, polished shoes, and took out the laundry for 5 dollars a week. It wasn't much, but he could stretch the wages with "Cumshaw." If Ketzler asked him to take something to the cleaners, the houseboy would come back and say it was one dollar, when it really only cost him 50 cents. The other 50 cents was considered Cumshaw. If Ketzler left out a pack of cigarettes, the houseboy would take eight of them because he didn't think Ketzler could smoke them all. Again, Cumshaw. Ketzler offered to pay him 10 dollars a week so he wouldn't have to steal, but he refused, saying, "That's not stealing, that's Cumshaw."

The French Tennis Club across the street from their hotel served as their mess hall. For the first three weeks, after they quit work around midnight, they ate dinner there. It was very fancy. The mens' and ladies' rest rooms didn't have plumbing, but they had beautifully decorated porcelain pots. There were rows, probably 20 on each side, of wooden seats over the pots. Everyone had his own individual pot, cleaned by the hired boys.

Ketzler and his men also liked to go to the Russian Club for dinner where they were served steaming bowls of soup. The soup was loaded with fat, which had been sorely lacking in their diet in China, so it tasted wonderful. The server would stir it into the soup just before he ladled it into their bowls. After a few spoonfuls, they chased the soup with shots of vodka. Ketzler said two men in his troop who got jaundice probably got it from trying to digest all that fat. They were also the only two who didn't drink the vodka. Ketzler thinks the vodka cut the grease so it didn't hurt his liver. To this day, he still thinks a glass of Vodka in the evening is helpful. However, he has never been able to get a doctor to confirm his theory.

Whenever Ketzler thinks of the movie *South Pacific,* he thinks of Shanghai. Every evening an old Chinese woman could be found sitting on the steps of the Grosner House where he lived. She spoke some English and he spoke a little Chinese, and he liked to go down in the evenings and talk with her. She had six younger Chinese girls with her. Men would come up and she would interrupt their conversation to negotiate a deal, send one of the girls off, and resume their conversation. Occasionally she inquired if Ketzler wanted to party. He said no, he just wanted to talk.

Ketzler's Austrian Jew interpreter was getting married and invited him to his wedding with a Chinese girl. The actual wedding ceremony was conducted by both a priest and the rabbi at the table and was very short, but the wedding banquet lasted over six hours. The guests ate and drank until they could hold no more, then left to lie down or take a walk. When they returned, there were served more food.

The Japanese invaded Shanghai in 1933 and were very brutal. They killed for the fun of killing and they ruled with an iron fist. They took over Shanghai and occupied it until after the end of WWII. The Chinese hadn't forgotten their brutality, and Shanghai was still full of Japanese civilians when Ketzler arrived. The Japanese men were held in prison camps, but the Japanese women were just restricted to certain areas of the city. The Chinese Nationalist soldiers liked to harass the women when they went out for errands. If they saw Japanese women on the street, they demanded an inspection. They were rough. Sometimes the women's groceries were knocked into the street. Ketzler witnessed this on his street one morning and yelled at the Chinese soldier, taunting him that he should come over and try and shake Ketzler down. The Chinese soldier was very intimidated and they avoided Ketzler's street after that.

Gordon McKinney, a cousin of Ketzler's mother, lived in Shanghai in 1933 and worked for the telephone company. When the Japanese attacked Shanghai, he sent his wife, Laura and daughter Mauveen, back to Omaha where they stayed with Ketzler's parents for the summer. In later years, McKinney showed Ketzler pictures of

Shanghai in the 1930s. One was of the front steps leading up to the Cathay mansion. When Ketzler was there, you walked right straight off the street into the hotel. It turned out that the Chinese gave the Europeans the lake bottom area for their buildings and the buildings were sinking.

Ketzler returned to Shanghai with Bette in 1990. They arrived by train at 9:00 on a rainy night and Ketzler didn't recognize anything. They walked up a flight of steps to their hotel room. He still didn't recognize it. When the couple went downstairs for dinner, they were told they would have to go across the street. Ketzler couldn't believe his eyes. It was the French Tennis Club. He then suddenly realized they were staying in Cathay Mansion, now called Jing Jang complex. The hotel was, indeed, the Cathay Mansion, which had sunk another full story – they had actually entered the mezzanine level. Ketzler asked the Chinese man at the door if this used to be the French Club. His eyes got wide and he said, "How you know? How you know?" Ketzler told him, this had been his mess hall during the war.

Even though the war with Japan was over, there was still a civil war going on between the Kuomintang (Nationalists) and the Chinese Communists. The Communists were at camps outside Shanghai, which was controlled by the Kuomintang. But when the Communists needed supplies, they sent their quartermasters into town to make the purchases. It was business as usual when it came to commerce.

Ketzler and his men continued working in Shanghai until things were well established. They turned the operation over the Chinese in December. Many of the American troops in the CBI were being sent home from that port and Mickey Landon stopped in to see Ketzler on his way home. Ketzler finally had orders to go home. He boarded the General Scott and sailed out of Shanghai on December 14.

Sailing Home

Sailing for America on an American ship with American food after more than two years in the CBI was cause for celebration. The first evening meal, the men were greeted by large baskets of freshly baked bread and tubs of butter – both of which had been non-existent in China. The men piled thick layers of butter on the bread. After the meal the ship's loudspeaker announced they were pleased the men liked the meal, but they had just consumed six day's rations of butter in one sitting.

Because there were still dangers on the sea, with many left over mines floating, the ships didn't cross the waters near Japan except during daylight. Two days out, the ship crossed near the southern tip of Japan. A watchman was posted with binoculars on the lookout for mines. It was a lazy sunny day and Ketzler had come up to hang over the bow of the ship where he could watch the flying fish and dolphins following along side. The bow hung way out over the water, so he could look straight down at the sea before the ship cut through the waves.

Suddenly, not eight feet from the bow, directly below him, Ketzler saw a floating mine. He could see the Japanese writing on it and its horns. He started yelling "Mine, Mine, Mine" and pointing down in front of the ship. The watchman yelled, "Where? Where?" and grabbed for the phone to call the pilot's room. But in his haste, he dropped the phone. Fortunately the ship's captain had seen the commotion and heeled the ship on its side, away from where Ketzler was pointing. The turning of the ship created a wave that kept pushing the mine away. It stayed about eight feet out from the ship, all the way along the side, until it passed by the stern. The ship circled and after several attempts with a 40 mm cannon, gunners finally blew the mine up. There was an enormous explosion. Ketzler thought, "The war is over and I almost got it for the second time."

It was Christmas Eve 1945, Ketzler's fourth as a Cavalryman. The ship encountered a large storm and pitched so violently that the men had to hold on to something at all times, or risk being thrown down. In the middle of the night the "Man Overboard" call was issued. Everyone scrambled for roll call. Ketzler was in charge of 30 men. He didn't know them, but had a roster. Quickly he determined they were all accounted for – as were all the other men on the ship. It turned out that a large trashcan had gone over board in the storm. It was a tense two hours.

* * *

The ship sailed into Puget Sound. It was a clear day with snow on the Olympic Mountains looking like melted ice cream sundaes. Ketzler could see Mt. Rainer and Mt. Baker on the mainland. It was the most beautiful sight he had ever seen. It took most of the day to get through the sound to the Seattle dock. He heard they were not going to allow anyone to take weapons off the ship, so he stood on deck and threw his .45, his ever-present companion, into the cold clear water. The ship docked about 9:00 that night. It was New Year's Eve.

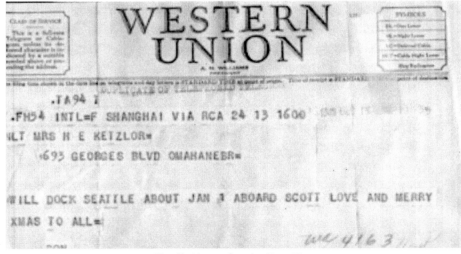

Finally Home for the New Year

Everyone was celebrating a safe homecoming. The atmosphere was jubilant. No one checked what the men took off the ship – they could have taken anything they wanted. Everyone just wanted to just go out and have a good time. Discovering that he could have kept his .45, Ketzler regretted throwing that pistol into the sound. He regrets it to this day.

Ketzler left the ship, went into a drug store and ordered a chocolate malt. Then he ordered another. After three chocolate malts he walked back to the ship and went to bed several hours before the West Coast rang in the New Year – 1946.

He called his parents New Year's Day. They had some very good friends, the McKinnons, who lived in Seattle. Later they came down to the ship, took Ketzler to dinner and, the next day drove him around the area. He lived on the ship in Seattle for three days. He then went to Fort Irwin in Seattle and boarded a train for Fort Lowery in Denver where he would be officially separated from the Army.

The first snow was falling as the train traveled through Wyoming. When the train stopped to let another train go through, and the men all jumped off. "Everyone was . . . having a blast," Ketzler said.

Chinese Medals Awarded to Ketzler

Flag for uniform to let Chinese know this was an Allied soldier

Patch of the Mars Task Force

U.S. Army Reserves

Everyone received the pitch to join the U.S. Army Reserves and Ketzler was no exception. He signed up. Back in Omaha, he reported to the Federal Building and was told they had a slot for him. Would he also like a commission? All he had to do was fill out some papers. It went before a board and he became Second Lieutenant Ketzler

He was originally put in an MP unit, but before long they established an Armored Cavalry unit in Omaha, at 22nd and Woolworth, in the old Kansas City warehouse. The headquarters was in Lincoln and they had another unit in Norfolk. He reported for duty where he was made lieutenant in charge of B Troop. Three months later he was made XO and in another six months, the captain retired and he took over the company.

The United States had entered into the Korean War and the Dehner Company was selling boots and uniforms to many of the Army officers. Ketzler discussed the war and the Army response with them when they came in to the factory. He learned that they were mostly sending over small units, which would then be broken up and the men sent to all different assignments. He was willing to take his Reserve unit over, but wanted them to stay together because they had worked together. The men agreed, so Ketzler decided they should join forces with a large unit that would be held together.

He contacted the 355th infantry, part of the 89th division that included Colorado and Nebraska with headquarters in Kansas. They had a regimental tank company, which his entire company could join. Omahan Jerry Givens served as commander. Ketzler remembers he was a great guy and a real go-getter. One of Ketzler's jobs was to supply him with a sergeant who would be his driver and assistant. Givens would wear one guy out by noon, so Ketzler would quickly have to find him another sergeant.

Givens had a trick knee, a result of a motorcycle accident. Every once in a while the knee would go out and he would be gone for a day or two. Ketzler would take over the company in his absence. When Givens was medically discharged, Ketzler was promoted to company commander, a post he held for seven years.

They were Cavalry, but a part of an Army infantry unit, and Ketzler kept seeing younger infantrymen promoted to the staff. Ketzler was doing a very good job as a tank company commander, but the infantry was taking care of its own. Ketzler was getting tired of it.

About that time he met a young West Pointer, Frances Winters, who had been in the Army for six or eight years. He wanted to go to law school, but the Army wouldn't send him, so he came back to Omaha to go to Creighton University Law School on his own. He was assigned to the Council Bluffs Reserves where he was giving everyone a fit. Ketzler thought he could get along with him and said he would take him on. He became Ketzler's XO.

"A lot of people are set on rules. I would see a guy who was doing a good job, so I didn't mind taking some heat for them," Ketzler said. For example he had a great big Lieutenant named Jack as his S-3. Ketzler remembers he could "belly out" anyone. When the troop headed to summer camp, Ketzler would figure out how much gas was needed and request that amount, but they would issue him about three-fourths of what was needed to keep their tanks going. When they were running out of gas, he sent Beno to get more. But he would come back empty handed. He sent a second man, a car salesman, but he also came back empty handed.

Finally, he sent Jack who came back with gas that he had "requisitioned" from some other unit. The men in the other unit were furious so Ketzler would smooth things over by telling the General he was really sorry and didn't have any idea his man was taking the gas. He said they had already used the gas but he would discipline Jack strongly.

Another example of Ketzler's belief that if you give a guy some latitude they can get something done. But if you are a hard ass – they probably won't.

Ketzler was troop commander over a tank company when he asked Winters to take over that company. Not long after they started up a unit about the size of a regiment, and Ketzler was asked if he wanted to be over it.

Ketzler was an S-3, Plans and Training, which is a key position. S-1 was Personnel; S-2 was Intelligence; S-3 was Plans and Training; and S-4 was Logistics. The chief of staff is actually the S-3 because he does the planning. "I had my little three shack. I had Beno and another assistant, Barrington. We got along very well," Ketzler remembers.

Ketzler was a horse cavalryman and loved horses, but he nearly as equally loved tanks. Although he never served in one, he did get to command them on maneuvers in the Reserves. One of the not-so-spectacular-moments in Ketzler's career took place at Fort Carson, Colorado. As tank commander of a large demonstration, he had been rigged with two phones, one phone to talk to the tanks and another that broadcast over the loud speaker, to explain the drill.

The huge tanks reached the spot where Ketzler had ordered them to turn left, but there was no response. They kept going straight. Ketzler yelled in the phone at them to turn, but still nothing happened. He remembers using a few choice words to try to get the attention of the tanks before he discovered that he was using the wrong phone. He had been yelling orders in not-so-polite language over the loudspeakers They quickly pulled the phone feeding into the loud speakers and Ketzler began commanding the tanks on the correct phone, while the General in charge explained how things don't always go as planned.

His reserve group had two tanks, a Sherman and a Patton, which were housed at Fort Omaha. To gas up, they drove the tanks into a gas station. It took about 200 gallons. The Patton tank was very heavy and was always breaking down. Fixing it was a major problem. Just to change the oil, you had to lift the engine out of the tank.

They would take the tanks out on maneuvers, sometimes heading north along Fort Calhoun road, which at that time, was Highway 75. One morning they were on Fort Calhoun Road next to Ponca Creek, where there was a small bridge with a weight limit of 10,000 pounds. The Sherman Tank weighed 34 tons and the Patton weighed 68 tons. They coasted over the bridge one at a time and made it just fine. However, on the way home, the Patton broke down and they had to tow it with chains, which put both tanks on the bridge at the same time. Ketzler ordered all but the drivers to get out. The two tanks then crossed very slowly. The bridge dropped about six inches. Once the tanks were off the bridge it came back up to within about two inches, but the supports were bent. As inconspicuously as could be done in two tanks, one being towed by the other, they left the scene as quickly as possible. Ketzler noted that a new bridge was built over Ponca Creek that year.

* * *

The Army had started an "Officers Career Management Program" in 1965. When they got to Ketzler, the man interviewing him said his file was incomplete. For example, it didn't mention where he had gone to college. Ketzler told him he hadn't gone to college. He asked him where he had gone to Officer Training School and Ketzler told him he hadn't gone to that either. In fact, Ketzler had been to none of the officers' training program that anyone of his rank should have attended. The man, in disbelief, asked him how he got to be a Major. Ketzler said he received Field Promotions. He was told that unless he got some education, his career was going nowhere.

So Ketzler signed up for correspondent courses. He took Junior Officer Training School and CandGS (Command and General Staff School), a graduate course, at the same time. With all the extra effort, he was going to about four summer camps a year. He took his wife and four children with him and they camped out while Van was in school.

He finished the required schools but was still passed over. The Army wasn't going to make him a Lt. Colonel. "They sent me a letter that said, 'Ketzler, you've done a wonderful job, and we don't know how we will run the Army without you, but starting tomorrow, we are going to try,'" Ketzler laughed.

Ketzler retired after 26 years in the U.S. Cavalry, with no regrets.

Epilogue

In looking back on his career in the reserves Ketzler said, "I think I was a good teacher because in the reserves, the men working under me did well. After I gave Frances Winterer my company, he was a Brigadier General in the National Guard within two years. Beno made 06 – Colonel. Barrington, one of my assistants, made Full Colonel. Another man, a Lieutenant, made full Colonel. If they worked for me they came out extremely well. But I never did make it to Colonel."

Ketzler, who turns 90 on Jan. 7, 2014, still rides his horse, Snow Drift several times a week, and rode with the North Hills (fox) Hunt until he was 87. In September 2005, he competed in jumping, military horsemanship and pistol shooting from horseback at a U.S. Cavalry reunion at Fort Robinson, Nebraska. He wasn't the oldest cavalryman at the event, but he was the oldest competing on horseback – by about 10 years.

Knowing his military history, some of his unique traits become clearly understandable.

- He always keeps a pistol nearby.
- He is extremely claustrophobic.
- It takes real persuasion to get him to fasten his seatbelt.
- He is prepared for virtually any emergency.
- When camping with his horse, he always positions the truck and trailer for a quick get-a-way if necessary.
- If he is told something can't be done, he probably will try to do it.
- He listens to the advice of experts, particularly in the medical field, but takes action according to his instincts. As a result, he is not a popular patient.

- He is always looking at his maps, and generally orders topographical maps of any area where he intends to travel off road.
- He judges every person individually and frequently employs handicapped, parolees, and minorities at his company.
- If something is broken, he fixes it…often with leather.
- He loves Chinese food and speaking Chinese to the servers.
- He has torn rotator cuffs four times, two on each arm, and all four times because he refused to let go of a horse he was leading.
- He loves a glass of vodka. An injury may require a shot of it. If he still hurts after the second glass, he will go to the emergency room.
- His favorite actor is John Wayne.

One day Ketzler was trail riding with five women, all several decades younger. As they were leaving the campground, a cowboy looked up from saddling his horse and asked him how he happened to have "all those beautiful women." Without missing a beat, Ketzler replied, "I only cut out of the herd what I can handle."

Appendix

U.S. Army, WWII
Timeline For the China Burma India Theater

- Early 1942 Stilwell was promoted to lieutenant general and tasked with establishing the CBI.
- February 25, 1942 Stilwell arrived in India by which time <u>Singapore</u> and <u>Burma</u> had both been invaded by the Japanese Army.
- March 10, 1942 Stilwell is named Chief of Staff of Allied armies in the Chinese theatre of operations.
- March 19, 1942 Stilwell's command in China is extended to include the Chinese 5th and 6th Armies operating in Burma after Chiang Kai-Shek gave his permission.
- March 20, 1942 Chinese troops under Stilwell engage Japanese forces along the Sittang River in Burma.
- April 9, 1942 <u>Claire Chennault</u> inducted into U.S. Army as a colonel, bringing the AVG <u>Flying Tigers</u> squadrons under Stilwell's nominal authority.
- April 16, 1942 7,000 British soldiers, and 500 prisoners and civilians were encircled by the <u>Japanese 33rd Division</u> at Yenangyaung.
- April 19, 1942 The 113th Regiment of the Chinese Expeditionary Force's New 38th Division led by General <u>Sun Li-jen</u> attacked and defeated the encircling Japanese troops rescuing the encircled British troops and civilians. This is historically called <u>Battle of Yenangyaung</u>.
- May 2, 1942 The commander of Allied forces in Burma, General <u>Harold Alexander,</u> ordered a general retreat to India. Instead of flying out, Stilwell remained with his troops and began a long retreat (he called it a "walk out") to India.
- May 24, 1942 Stilwell arrived in Delhi. Most of his Chinese troops had deserted.

- New Delhi and Ramgarh became the main training centre for Chinese troops in India. Chiang Kai-Shek gave Stilwell command of what was left of the 22nd and 38th Divisions of the Chinese Army.

- December 1, 1942 British General Sir <u>Archibald Wavell</u>, as Allied Supreme Commander South East Asia, agreed with Stilwell to make the <u>Ledo Road</u> an American operation.[16]

- August 1943 US creates a jungle <u>commando</u> unit, similar to the <u>Chindits</u>, to be commanded by Major General <u>Frank Merrill</u>; it is informally called "Merrill's Marauders".[17]
- Exhaustion and disease led to the early evacuation of many Chinese and American troops before the coming assault on Myitkyina.[18]
- December 21 Stilwell assumed direct control of operations to capture <u>Myitkyina</u>, having built up forces for an offensive in Northern Burma.
- February 24, 1944 <u>Merrill's Marauders</u>, attacked the Japanese 18th Division in Burma. This action enabled Stilwell to gain control of the <u>Hakawing Valley</u>.

- May 17, 1944 British general <u>Slim</u> in command of the <u>Burma Campaign</u> handed control of the Chindits to Stilwell.
- May 17, 1944 Chinese troops, with the help of Merrill's Mauraders, captured Myitkina airfield.
- August 3, 1944 Myitkina fell to the Allies. The Mauraders had advanced 750 miles and fought in five major engagements and 32 skirmishes with the Japanese Army. They lost 700 men, only 1,300 Marauders reached their objective and of these, 679 had to be hospitalized. This included General Merrill who had suffered a second-heart attack before going down with malaria.
- Some time before August 27, 1944, <u>Mountbatten</u> supreme allied commander (SEAC) ordered General Stilwell to evacuate all the wounded Chindits.

- During 1944 the Japanese in <u>Operation Ichi-Go</u> overran US air bases in eastern China. Chiang Kai-Shek blamed Stilwell for the Japanese success, and pressed the US high command to recall him.
- October 1944 Roosevelt recalled Stilwell, whose role was split (as was the CBI):
  - Lieutenant General <u>Raymond Wheeler</u> became Deputy Supreme Allied Commander South East Asia.

- Major General <u>Albert Wedemeyer</u> became Chief of Staff to *Chiang Kai-shek* and commander of the U.S. Forces, China Theater (USFCT).[19]
- Lieutenant General <u>Daniel Sultan</u> was promoted from deputy commander to became commander of US Forces India-Burma Theater (USFIBT) and commander of the <u>Northern Combat Area Command</u>

- January 12, 1945, the first convoy over the <u>Ledo Road</u> of 113 vehicles led by General <u>Pick</u> from <u>Ledo</u> reached <u>Kunming</u>, China on February 4, 1945. Over the next seven months 35,000 tons of supplies in 5,000 vehicles were carried along it.[20]

CPSIA information can be obtained at www.ICGtesting.com
Printed in the USA
BVOW05s1804240414

351630BV00007B/55/P